FROM THE EAST OF CHINA
comes food well cooked, with dark sauces and rich,
pungent flavors

FROM THE WEST OF CHINA
come hot and spicy dishes to tingle the taste buds
and stir the appetite

FROM THE SOUTH OF CHINA
come crisp-cooked vegetables and inimitably subtle
delicacies

FROM THE NORTH OF CHINA
come marvelous dumplings and noodle dishes

You will find all regions represented in one cook-
book that combines the ancient wisdom of the
Orient with the modern know-how of Western
technology.

CHINESE COOKING THE EASY WAY
with Food Processors

CHINESE COOKING THE EASY WAY
with Food Processors

Dee Wang

POPULAR LIBRARY • NEW YORK

CHINESE COOKING THE EASY WAY
WITH FOOD PROCESSORS

Published by Popular Library, a unit of CBS Publications, the Consumer Publishing Division of CBS Inc.

This book contains the complete text of the original hardcover edition.

ISBN: 0-445-04474-8

Printed in the United States of America

First Popular Library printing: October 1979

10   9   8   7   6   5   4   3   2   1

This book is dedicated to my father, who is resting in heaven. He cultivated my taste and taught me to appreciate good food.

I want to thank Charlotte Gordon, Irene Copeland, and my two daughters-in-law, Julia and Rebecca, who helped me to put this book together.

Contents

Introduction

I consider myself fortunate to have been born in Shanghai, China, some fifty years ago. Shanghai, a seaport on China's east coast, was then something like Manhattan—a cosmopolitan city. People of many different nationalities lived there, and there were good restaurants serving the cuisines of France, Germany, and Russia. Needless to say, there were countless restaurants specializing in foods from all parts of China as well. It was a gourmet's heaven.

I was born into a big family. My grandfather had passed away long before, and my grandmother ruled the household. Her four sons and their families all lived under one roof. We had two chefs and nine other servants, and when the servants weren't cleaning, they were always involved in food preparation for special projects. One day it might be sausage making; another time the creation of festive cakes. Our family came from the southern province of Kwong Tung, where good eating was rated as most important. Dinner at home was always a two-hour affair, and trying out new restaurants was a favorite pastime. So I was exposed to good food at an early age.

My father had an extraordinary interest in cooking and eating, and he loved to develop new dishes. He set up his own little kitchen and experimented with creating his own recipes, which he would perfect and then turn over to the chefs. It was customary at that time not to allow young girls into the kitchen; but my father's domain was a different territory, so I could watch and help. It was there that I first learned how to make Shrimp Toast and Curried Crescents. It was there that I learned the fundamental rules of cooking.

After World War II I got married and came to the United States with my husband, who was studying for his master's degree. We set up housekeeping, and I began to put my cooking lessons to use. We lived first in Albuquerque, New Mexico, and then in Denver, Colorado. During those three years in the Southwest, we were unable to get authentic Chinese ingredients, so I had to improvise with what I found in the supermarkets. It was often quite a challenge.

When we moved to the New York area, I was overwhelmed by the availability of authentic cooking utensils and ingredients. It became much easier to cook an assortment of provincial dishes to satisfy the whole family. In fact, we *had* to cook a tremendous variety to keep everyone content. My husband was born in Peking and favored the northern cuisine; his parents, who lived with us, were born in the eastern region and preferred that style of cooking; our housekeeper, who was born in the western region, favored her own dishes. It was wonderful to have so many cooking styles represented at meals.

After my three sons left for college, I had much time on my hands. My friend, Mrs. Florence Lin, who is well known in Chinese cookery, encouraged me to teach Chinese cooking, as she did. Thus I started my new career, which has been a truly rewarding experience. Cooking is a nice way to express one's love for people, and I was happy to teach my students new dishes and so help them give their families enjoyment.

I believe the basic principles are the most important thing. Once you have learned the basic cooking techniques, you can use your imagination to vary them to suit your family's taste and needs. You don't have to know how to cook thousands of dishes; just master the ones that you and your family like.

There are literally thousands of recipes from China to choose from, in four major cooking styles. In the northern regions, where wheat is grown, flour rather than rice is the main staple, so dumplings, steamed breads, and noodle dishes are specialties. Easterners like their food well cooked, with dark soy sauce and often some sugar among the ingredients. In the western regions spicy-hot foods are preferred with flavors similar to Mexican cooking. Southerners like crisp-cooked vegetables and subtle flavors. I have chosen many of my favorite recipes, some from each of the four regional cuisines, to share with you.

You may find that the recipes are a little different from those you are used to. I never use monosodium glutamate in any recipe, although many Chinese cooks do. Animal fat is reduced to the very minimum, and very few dairy products are used. If you follow my custom of allowing only four ounces of meat for each serving, and use corn oil for cooking, you will consistently serve low-cholesterol meals to your family. You will enjoy good food and help avoid health problems at the same time.

1
Read This First!

Basic Techniques

What makes Chinese food Chinese lies essentially in the way it is prepared before cooking, and the actual methods of cooking. The two are closely allied—for example, meat and vegetables are sliced or shredded in special ways so that they will cook quickly in that most Chinese of cooking methods, stir-frying. In this section you will learn all about these techniques. And they will soon become second nature to you.

SLICING MEAT
With the food processor. For Chinese cooking slices should be small, almost bite-size, so the processor is the ideal tool. Cut meat in chunks that will fit the feed tube. For maximum tenderness be sure to cut so that the machine will slice across the grain. Freeze the chunks until the meat is firm but can be pierced with a knife. Or partially defrost frozen meat to the same stage. With the slicing disk in place, put a chunk of meat in the tube and

process with pressure. The result will be ⅛-inch-thick slices. Repeat until all of the meat has been sliced.

With a knife. Use a sharp knife or cleaver and always cut across the grain. Again, meat will be easier to slice if it is partially frozen. Make chunks about 2 inches by ¾ inch and slice ⅛ inch thick.

SLICING VEGETABLES

With the food processor. Firm vegetables like carrots, bamboo shoots, turnips, broccoli stems, and celery are no problem at all for the slicing disk of the processor. Always use pressure, so slices do not come out too thin.

With a knife. If you use a knife, you can cut vegetables in designs that are most appealing in shape. One very attractive and easy technique is diagonal cutting— simply slice at an angle. Roll-cutting, a variation of diagonal cutting, is a little more difficult. Make a diagonal cut at about a thirty-degree angle, roll the vegetable a quarter turn, and make another thirty-degree-angle cut. Continue cutting and rolling until vegetable is completely sliced. You should get little triangular pieces. See diagram on page 32.

DICING MEAT

With a knife. To "dice" means making little squares no bigger than ⅜ inch. Meat should be partially frozen, then sliced ⅜ inch thick. Stack 2 or 3 slices and cut again into ⅜-inch strips. Now hold a few strips together and cut across, into ⅜-inch squares.

DICING VEGETABLES

With a knife. Make ⅜-inch slices, stack 2 or 3 slices, and cut again into ⅜-inch strips. Holding a few strips together, cut across into ⅜-inch squares.

SHREDDING MEAT

With the food processor. Cut partially frozen meat across the grain into ⅛-inch slices measuring about 2 inches by 3 inches. Stack 4 or 5 slices and, with the slicing disk in place, stand them on edge in the feed tube. Process with pressure to get uniform shreds.

With a knife. Cut partially frozen meat across the grain into ⅛-inch-thick slices. Stack 4 or 5 slices and cut shreds ⅛ inch wide.

SHREDDING VEGETABLES

With the food processor. The shredding disk is perfect for firm vegetables like carrots, bamboo shoots, and turnips. With leafy vegetables like cabbage, Chinese cabbage, or bok choy it is best to use the slicing disk.

With a knife. Slice, stack, and slice again into ⅛-inch shreds. Shred along the grain rather than across it; the shreds will look better and hold their shape better.

MINCING MEAT

With the food processor. Cut partially frozen meat into 1-inch cubes. Put them into the work bowl with the steel blade. (Refreeze if they have defrosted.) Mince by switching the motor on and off quickly a few times. Be careful not to overprocess.

With a knife. Shred as described above, then stack several shreds together and cut crosswise into ⅛-inch bits.

MINCING VEGETABLES

With the food processor. Put the 1½-inch pieces into the work bowl with the steel blade and turn the motor on and off quickly. Watch carefully to avoid overprocessing or you will wind up with a vegetable puree.

With a knife. Slice vegetables thin, then pile them up and chop quickly, first in one direction and then the other. As you chop, keep changing direction and scooping the vegetables into a pile with the knife.

THICKENING

Mix cornstarch with cold liquid and add gradually to a sauce or gravy to thicken it. Do not add all at once or you may thicken the sauce more than you meant to. Be sure to stir the cornstarch mixture immediately before using it.

BLANCHING

This is a process of passing food through boiling water. Blanching vegetables helps shorten the cooking time later. Simply place them in boiling water and remove when the water returns to a boil. Blanching meat, fish, seafood, and poultry cleans them and removes unpleasant odors.

STIR-FRYING

This technique is unique to Chinese cooking. The object is to cook food quickly in a small amount of oil over high heat, to seal in the flavor and juices. Here's how:

1. Use sufficient heat. With an electric range, set on medium high or high and wait for the coils to become reddish before putting the wok or pan on the heat. I usually put a kettle of water on the coils while they are heating to prevent accidental burns. With a gas range, turn the flame up high and put the wok directly over it.

2. Do not use the ring that comes with the wok during stir-frying unless your wok is not stable. It elevates the wok and allows less heat to reach the food.

3. Be sure the wok is absolutely dry before putting the oil in. Otherwise the moisture will make the oil splatter. This can be dangerous as well as messy.

4. Always wait until the oil is hot before putting the food in. The temperature should be about 350 to 400 degrees F. Test by holding your hand about 12 inches above the oil. If you can feel the heat, the temperature is right. Or put a large garlic clove or slice of ginger in the oil. When it turns brown the temperature is right for stir-frying.

5. Always cut meat and vegetables into small, uniform slices. If two or more vegetables go into the wok at

one time, firmer ones should be cut smaller or thinner than soft ones so they cook in the same amount of time.

6. Never put more than 2 cups of meat in a wok or pan to stir-fry. With too much meat, heat will be reduced, and you will be stewing instead of stir-frying.

7. Stir continuously as you fry, spreading the food around the wok and then turning it in toward the center. Keep on spreading and turning until done.

STEAMING

This is a process of cooking in the steam produced by boiling water. You must always steam over high heat, to keep the water boiling. Add more boiling water as it evaporates. The traditional Chinese steamer is a pot with a cover and perforated trays that stack. Two or three foods can steam at the same time.

You can also use a wok for steaming. Put in a rack that fits halfway up and top with a high cover. Or use any large pot or a turkey roaster. Put the food in a heat-proof dish, set on the rack, and cover.

Utensils

You probably already own enough utensils to cook fabulous Chinese meals. By adding a few traditional items you can have a really well-equipped Chinese kitchen.

KNIFE

A sharp knife not only makes cutting easier—it is safer to use as well. If you have to struggle with a dull knife, you are much more likely to cut yourself. A good French chef's knife will do the job. Even better is a Chinese cleaver. The back of the rectangular blade is broad enough to be used as a meat tenderizer. The wide blade can scoop up food from the chopping board. When you buy a cleaver, test its weight in your hand, and choose the one that feels most comfortable. Blades come in different thicknesses. The thin blade can slice and chop meat; the thicker blade can also chop through chicken bones and thin meat bones. I have both kinds in my kitchen; but if you don't plan to cut bones, choose only the thinner blade.

FOOD PROCESSOR

This versatile machine can take over much of the work of the knife or cleaver, and do many jobs in seconds that might otherwise be difficult or extremely time consuming. Because there is so much chopping and slicing in Chinese food preparation, a processor is ideal for this cuisine.

THE STEEL BLADE CAN

Chop vegetables and meat. Always chop by switching the motor on and off. Meat should be partially frozen. All food that goes into the work bowl should be cut in uniform pieces.

Mince vegetables and meat. Process as for chopping, but for a slightly longer time. Be careful not to overprocess.

Puree vegetables and meat. Turn the motor on and process until a pastelike mass is formed.

Knead dough. Put the dry ingredients in the work bowl. Turn on the motor and add liquid gradually through the feed tube while continuing to process until a ball of dough forms. At this point the dough is ready.

THE SLICING DISK CAN

Slice meat. Partially freeze or defrost meat to the point at which a knife can just penetrate. Cut chunks to fit the feed tube and slice across the grain, using pressure for uniform slices.

Slice vegetables. Vegetables do not need to be frozen. They can be sliced any way you want.

Shred meat and vegetables. Slice, then stack slices, place on edge in the feed tube, and process. To shred cabbage, cut chunks and process with a little pressure with the slicing dish.

Slice scallions. To chop just one scallion, hold it upright by the end and, with the slicing disk in place, feed it through the tube without using the pusher. Keep your hand out of the feed tube. To chop a bunch of scallions, cut them to the length of the tube, fasten at the top with a rubber band and stand them up in the tube. Use the pusher to process with pressure. If you are careful, you can stop before the rubber band hits the disk. If you miss, simply pick the rubber band out of the work bowl.

THE SHREDDING DISK CAN
Shred firm vegetables like carrots, bamboo shoots, cucumbers, potatoes, turnips, and ginger root. Make sure you shred with the grain, not across.

WOK
The chief advantage of the wok is its shape. A pot or frying pan can be used instead, but the wok's rounded bottom lets you work with either a small or large amount of food and still turn, stir, and toss it easily. Woks come in a range of sizes and styles. A 12-inch wok will be suitable for a family of two to four. A 14-inch wok lets you cook dishes to serve six or eight people, and is probably the most versatile size. If you often cook for a crowd, you may need a 16-inch wok, but buy it only if the burners on your stove are far enough apart to accommodate the wok on one and still allow you to use the others.

A wok with a wooden handle will be a bit more expensive, but the handle is a worthwhile convenience. You can use it to steady the wok while cooking, and you won't need a pot holder. A stainless-steel wok is more expensive, but beautiful. I have found that food sticks readily in stainless steel, but it heats up evenly and fast and is therefore excellent for deep-fat frying. A Teflon-coated electric wok allows you to use less oil in cooking. You can bring it to the table and serve from it, and keep food warm in it. It also acts as an extra burner in a busy kitchen, and you can stir-fry at the table if you like. The only drawback is that it doesn't get hot enough to handle a large amount of food.

A wok can last a lifetime if you take care of it properly. Some cooks prefer just to wash off the wok with soap and water. This allows a coating of cooked-on oil to build up and season the wok so food doesn't stick. I prefer to scrub my wok each time I use it. I set it over low heat to dry, then wipe it with a few drops of oil on a paper towel to make sure it doesn't rust. The ring that comes with the wok should not be used during cooking, as it elevates the wok too far from the heat—unless, of course, your wok needs steadying. It is useful, though, for resting the wok when you are not cooking. The cover of the wok is used for steaming, stewing, and simmering.

TEFLON-COATED PAN

I always keep one Teflon-coated pan on hand for cooking noodles, pasta, and rice dishes, which would ordinarily stick without a lot of oil. With the Teflon pan you can reduce the amount of oil and still get crisp noodles or wontons.

SLOTTED SPOON

The shape fits the wok better than the traditional Chinese spatula, and since it is slotted, you can lift food and drain off any excess oil. It is also useful for lifting blanched foods from boiling water. If you use a Teflon-coated electric wok, you need a slotted spoon made of plastic to avoid scratching the Teflon coating.

CHOPSTICKS

I cannot cook without them. Chopsticks serve as a fork, a wooden spoon, and wooden tongs. Once you master the use of chopsticks, you will find them indispensable.

CAKE RACKS

A 10-inch cake rack with ¾-inch legs will fit in your

wok for steaming, and can also be used to dry out foods like wontons or the duck for the Peking Duck recipe. An 8-inch rack with 2-inch legs is useful for steaming food in your turkey roaster or a large pot. When steaming, always use a plate to hold the food on the rack.

Available Ingredients

You can prepare many, many Chinese dishes without going any farther than your neighborhood supermarket for the ingredients. The freshness and quality of produce and meat, fish, and poultry are what counts, and the staple ingredients you will use in nearly every dish—like soy sauce, corn oil, and cornstarch—are truly universal.

SOY SAUCE

Soy sauce is brewed of soybeans, wheat, salt, and water. The Chinese make two varieties, a dark soy that is thick and slightly less salty, and a light soy, thinner and more salty. Each has its special place in the cuisine of different regions. Japanese soy sauce is a medium soy, and it is the one I use in all of my recipes. The brand I prefer is Kikkoman, and since it is available almost everywhere, I suggest you try it also. Kikkoman soy sauce comes in two varieties, regular, which contains 17 percent salt, and low-salt, with 8 percent salt. An equally good Japanese soy sauce is the Yamasa brand. Soy sauce has a distinctive flavor that people associate with Oriental food. It is used both in preparing food and as an additional seasoning. It keeps indefinitely and does not have to be refrigerated.

OIL

Oil is essential for stir-frying, sautéing, pan-frying, and deep-frying. Cooking in hot oil helps seal in the juices and flavor of food. There are many types. My personal choice is corn oil (Mazola brand) because it is polyunsaturated and therefore low in cholesterol. Safflower oil is even higher in polyunsaturates, but it has a faint odor. Peanut oil is a good odorless oil, but quite a bit lower in polyunsaturates than corn oil. Other vegetable oils have an odor when heated and therefore are not recommended for Chinese cooking. The following list compares the level of polyunsaturates in various types of cooking oil:

Safflower oil	75	Olive oil	7
Mazola corn oil	61	Butter	4
Cottonseed oil	52	Coconut oil	1
Peanut oil	31	Specially processed	
Chicken fat	27	soybean oil	37

CHICKEN BROTH

A good-quality chicken stock improves the flavor of any dish. Ideally, you should make your own from fresh chicken or chicken bones (see page 60). The next best is a good canned broth. My choice is College Inn. Third best are chicken-broth cubes dissolved in water. Knorr's chicken-broth cubes are the closest to homemade broth.

CORNSTARCH

This versatile ingredient is used three ways in Chinese cooking: as a thickener, in marinades, and as a coating for deep-frying. (Some people prefer to use arrowroot because they think it has fewer calories. Actually the calorie count per tablespoon for each is identical—29. Arrowroot is more expensive and does the job no better than cornstarch.)

To thicken sauces. Cornstarch is the ideal thickener for sauces, soups, and gravies because it makes a clear sauce—unlike flour, which makes a cloudy one. A tablespoon of cornstarch has the thickening power of 2 tablespoons of flour. Mix cornstarch with cold water or other liquid and add very gradually to the sauce to be thickened, stirring while you add it. In this way you can stop as soon as the sauce reaches the desired thickness. Always stir the cornstarch mixture before using it, as it has a tendency to settle.

To hold a marinade. When you marinate meat, cornstarch helps to hold the liquid in the meat. Then, when you stir-fry or cook it, the flavor and juices will be sealed in, and the meat will be flavorful and tender.

To coat food for frying. When you deep-fry food, roll the pieces in cornstarch first. The result will be a very crunchy coating. You can prove this by trying the Fried Chicken Chinese Style, page 92, and the Sweet-and Sour Pork, page 112.

WHITE PEPPER

White pepper is used instead of black pepper because it is finely ground and does not show up in food as black pepper would. It is also a little milder.

SALT

I try to keep my recipes in the middle range, neither too salty nor too bland. However, it is easy to add to or reduce the amount of salt according to your taste. I prefer Diamond brand because it seems a little less salty to me. Coarse salt, like kosher salt, is useful for salting food prior to cooking, but it should not be used as a seasoning during cooking.

MEAT

Always choose the freshest meat possible. It should be red in color; if it looks a little grayish, it is not fresh. When I buy meat, I always trim off the fat and then cut it into portion-size pieces so I can keep it in the freezer and defrost only as much as I need. Always save all meat bones and store them in the freezer until you have enough to make a soup stock.

Beef. Flank steak, sirloin, and fillet are all very tender cuts for slicing and shredding. Top round or bottom round are also suitable if you use a little unflavored meat tenderizer.

Pork. Pork tenderloin, the loin part of pork chops,

is excellent for slicing and shredding. Trim off all fat. Chicken breast or veal can be used interchangeably in recipes calling for this cut of pork.

Veal. Veal is more expensive than beef and pork. I have not included any veal recipes in this book, but the loin part of veal and the scallopine cut can be used in any of the chicken and pork recipes.

Chicken. Fresh-killed chickens are the best, but they are not always available. Be sure to choose plump, meaty chickens with a nice clean skin. Chicken parts are convenient, but you will save money if you buy whole chickens and cut them into pieces for use in different recipes. Save the bones to make soup.

Fish. When you buy a whole fish, examine its eyes and gills. The eyes should protrude a little and be bright and shiny, not dried out. The gills should be pink or reddish, not slimy. When you buy fish fillets, the flesh should be firm and the skin side shiny.

Shrimp. Fresh shrimp in the shell are the best. Examine to make sure the shells are hard and firmly attached to the shrimp. I prefer a slightly bluish tinge to the shells. If you freeze the shrimp with the shells on, they will be just as good when they are defrosted. Without the shells, they lose a lot of their natural moisture when you defrost them. Frozen shrimp, sold cleaned and deveined, are easy to use but they are not as good. In some recipes they should definitely *not* be used: I will tell you when.

VEGETABLES

Choose vegetables that are crisp, not dried out or wilted. Leaves should be unblemished and stems firm, not flabby. If you do not use vegetables the same day, store them, unwashed, in brown paper bags, rolled up tight, then in plastic bags. The paper will absorb the moisture, and the vegetables should stay fresh for two or three days in the refrigerator.

LOW-FAT FOODS

For those of you who are interested in the cholesterol content of various foods, here is a comparison, in milligrams per 100 grams (3½ ounces), of many popular foods, from the University of Iowa's *Low Cholesterol Diet Manual:*

Scallops	166	*Haddock*	64
Shrimp	161	*Perch*	63
Lobster	83	*Pork tenderloin*	57
Chicken (dark meat)	76	*Trout*	57
Veal	71	*Salmon*	55
Pike	71	*Chicken (white meat)*	54
Beef round steak	68	*Vegetables*	0
Lamb chop	66	*Egg white*	0

Glossary of Authentic Chinese Ingredients

These prepared sauces and special ingredients are becoming more and more available, especially in large cities, and even in some neighborhood supermarkets. Some Chinese groceries will fill mail orders. You should become familiar with these ingredients and try to use them when you can. They will add a special touch to your cooking.

AGAR-AGAR
This is a gelatin derived from a vegetable. It is very different from animal gelatins like Knox and Jell-O. Instead of a powder, it comes in a solid rectangle or in long, fine strips like noodles, and must be boiled to dissolve.

BAMBOO SHOOTS
In this country bamboo shoots are available only in cans. Supermarkets usually carry sliced bamboo shoots in 8-ounce cans. In Oriental groceries you can buy canned chunks and other shapes. Once you open the can, drain and refrigerate the bamboo shoots in a jar of fresh water. Covered, and with a change of water daily, they should keep for a week or more.

BEAN CURD

Sold by the cake in Chinese groceries, bean curd is made from soybeans. (See page 153.) Store as you would store bamboo shoots.

BEAN SAUCE

Made from soybeans and soy sauce, bean sauce is pasty and brown with pieces of bean in it. It comes in cans or jars. Sold only in Oriental stores.

BOK CHOY

This is a leafy vegetable, a type of cabbage, which looks very much like Swiss chard.

BROWN VINEGAR

Use Chengkong Vinegar, which comes from the People's Republic of China, in 21-fluid-ounce bottles.

CELERY CABBAGE

The stem end looks like celery, the leafy part more like cabbage. Now becoming available in some supermarkets, it can be used instead of bok choy.

CELLOPHANE NOODLES

When cooked, these noodles become translucent—which explains their name. They are made from a puree of mung beans and are therefore high in protein. When dried, they become very stiff, like wire, but after you soak and cook them they become soft. Some cooks deep-fry the dry noodles. They puff in a second and turn white, and make a beautiful garnish. You will find them in 2-ounce, 8-ounce, and 1-pound packages in Oriental stores.

CHINESE BLACK MUSHROOMS

These dried mushrooms are sold by weight or in cellophane packages in Oriental stores. They must be soaked in water for at least an hour before using. The stems are tough and should be discarded. Chinese mushrooms are expensive, but since you use only a few in each recipe, they last a long time. Two tablespoons of dried mushrooms are equivalent to ½ cup fresh.

CHINESE BROCCOLI

Similar to American broccoli, this is a green vegetable with a main stem, a few leaves, and little flowers. You eat the stem and leaves of Chinese broccoli but not the flowers.

CORIANDER

You will find this very fragrant parsley in Italian groceries (where it is known as *cilantro*) and in some American markets (sometimes called Chinese parsley), as well as in Oriental stores.

DRIED SEAWEED

Dried and pressed into sheets, seaweed is very easy to use. It is sold wrapped in cellophane in Oriental stores. Just break the sheet into small pieces and add to soup. Seaweed is a good iodine source.

DRIED SHRIMP

These are fresh shrimp that have been salted, cooked, and sun-dried so they can be kept for a long time. If you have a cool storage place, they do not need refrigeration. They are usually soaked before being added to a dish for extra flavor, and are widely used in authentic Chinese cooking. They are not to be used as a substitute for fresh shrimp.

GINGER ROOT

Fresh ginger root is sold by weight in Oriental and some American groceries. It keeps for 2 to 3 weeks at a cool room temperature, or in the refrigerator wrapped in paper towels to absorb excess moisture. You can even cut the tuber in thin slices and freeze it. Ginger is used sparingly because it has a very decided flavor, spicy with a sharp tang. In seafood dishes it helps to take away the fishy odor.

GLUTINOUS RICE
Also called sweet rice, glutinous rice is short-grained and becomes sticky when cooked. It is not eaten plain like regular rice, but is used as an ingredient in Chinese pastries.

HOISIN SAUCE
This is another sauce made from soybeans, soy sauce, spices, and sugar. It is a smooth, thick brown paste, and it is sold in cans or jars. Once opened, it should be stored in the refrigerator, where it will keep for months.

HOT CHILI OIL
You can buy this reddish oil at Oriental stores, or you can make your own simply by heating oil and crushed pepper flakes together for at least 10 minutes, then straining into a bottle. This oil will stay fresh for a long time.

JUJUBE
This is a red Chinese date with a skin that is thicker than the regular date. It is usually used puréed, as a filling in desserts.

LUNG-AN
Similar to the lichee, this very sweet fruit is the size of a large cherry. It has a brown pit, white meat, and a beige skin. Lung-an come packed in syrup in cans, or dried like dates.

MUNG BEANS
If you let these beans sprout (see page 155) they become—bean sprouts. Pureed, these tiny green beans are used to make cellophane noodles.

NAPA CABBAGE
This variety of celery cabbage gets its name from the Napa Valley in California, where it is cultivated. Napa cabbage is shorter, rounder, and more flavorful than celery cabbage.

OYSTER SAUCE
Similar to brown gravy, this sauce is made of oysters steamed with soy sauce, then thickened with cornstarch. I strongly recommend one brand, Hop Sing Lung. There are many inferior ones.

RED BEAN PASTE
This sweetened puree of red beans, available in cans, is a standard filling for Chinese and Japanese pastries.

RICE FLOUR
Since rice is the main staple of the Orient, rice flour is as popular there as wheat flour is in the Western world.

SALTED BLACK BEANS
These fermented soybeans are salty and very pungent. They are found in Oriental stores in cans or packages (I prefer the packages) and are used as seasoning. Since they are salted, they need no refrigeration. Keep them in a tightly covered jar.

SESAME-SEED OIL
The oil found in Oriental stores is very sharp in flavor and is used as a flavoring rather than a cooking oil. It keeps indefinitely without refrigeration. Sesame-seed oil from health-food stores is quite different: it is lighter, has less flavor, is more expensive, and needs refrigeration after opening. When sesame-seed oil is called for in my recipes, the Oriental type should be used.

SESAME-SEED OIL WITH CHILI
This is a reddish sesame-seed oil heated with chili and strained. Sold in bottles in Chinese groceries, it is very fiery.

STAR ANISE
This dried spice, which looks like a star, is the source of anise powder. In Oriental cooking it takes the place of bay leaf.

SZE-CHUAN HOT BEAN SAUCE

This spicy sauce is made of fermented bean paste and chili paste.

SZE-CHUAN PEPPERCORNS

More spicy and aromatic than familiar black peppercorns, these have a taste that is sharper. Used especially in Sze-Chuan cooking.

TAPIOCA FLOUR

The same as tapioca starch, tapioca flour is ground from the cassava root.

TIGER-LILY BUDS

These are the dried buds of an especially large tiger lily. They must be soaked for about an hour before using. Very delicate in flavor, they are almost always used along with tree ears.

TREE EARS

Also called cloud ears and tree fungus, tree ears, a good source of protein, are a form of fungus that grows on trees. They are sold dried and must be soaked before use. When soaked, they can swell to six times their dried volume. Their gelatinous texture is what makes them an intriguing addition to a dish.

WATER CHESTNUTS

Fresh water chestnuts are available only from Oriental stores. Grown under water, they are sweet and juicy like fruit, with a crunchy texture. Peel the brown coating before use. Supermarkets carry canned water chestnuts, which are cooked, peeled, and ready to eat. They are not as sweet as fresh ones, but still crunchy.

WHEAT STARCH

Wheat flour without gluten is wheat starch. It is sold like regular flour in sacks.

WHITE SESAME SEEDS

These are sold in Oriental stores and also in health-food stores, where they are not as white as the Oriental ones.

WINTER MELON

The flesh of a winter melon has a texture like squash, but in size it resembles a watermelon or pumpkin. The outside skin is dark green, the flesh is white, and when cooked it becomes translucent. Only available in Oriental stores when in season, it is sold by the pound, so you don't have to buy the whole melon.

WONTON WRAPPERS

These are sheets of dough made of flour, water and egg. They are found in Oriental stores in packages of 60 to 80. Each paper-thin sheet measures about 2½ inches square.

ONE STYLE OF WONTON

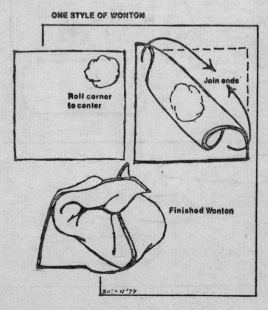

Roll corner to center

Join ends

Finished Wonton

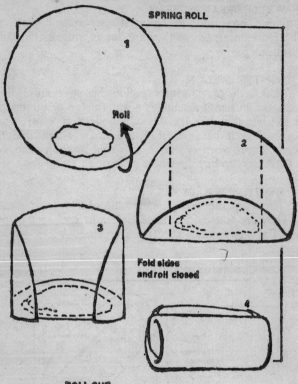

SPRING ROLL

Roll

Fold sides
and roll closed

ROLL-CUT

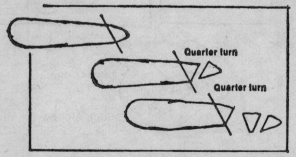

Quarter turn

Quarter turn

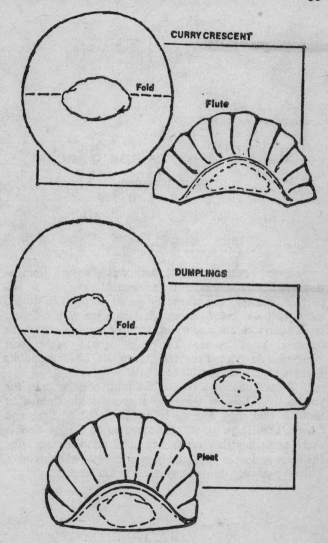

CURRY CRESCENT

Fold

Flute

DUMPLINGS

Fold

Pleat

2
Hors d'Oeuvres and Snacks

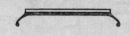

When I was in China, there was always a tremendous variety of snacks. People regarded eating as an important business, and whenever guests dropped in during the day, it was courteous to offer them tea with different types of snacks, salty or sweet, so most families kept some on hand at all times. The salty snacks make great Western-style hors d'oeuvres. Many are bite-size tidbits that are ideal to serve with cocktails.

I have chosen a few of the most popular ones for you to try. The best thing about them, aside from their taste, is that they can all be made ahead of time and frozen. Line them up without touching on a large cookie sheet, and when they are frozen solid, remove them from the sheet and store in plastic bags or in covered containers. This way you can defrost any number you need.

Shrimp Toast
8 Servings

Everyone has his favorite style of Shrimp Toast. I like mine light and crisp. Besides serving as one of the traditional first courses in a banquet menu, it is tops as an hors d'oeuvre. You must use only fresh shrimp, not frozen.

8 water chestnuts*	1 egg
1 pound fresh shrimp, cleaned and deveined	1 tablespoon corn oil
1 scallion	8 thin slices of white bread
1 teaspoon salt	¼ cup white sesame seeds
	Corn oil for deep-frying
	⅛ teaspoon white pepper

PROCESSING
Put the water chestnuts in the work bowl with the steel blade and mince by turning the motor on and off quickly once or twice. Remove to a regular bowl. Put in the shrimp and process to a paste. Put in the bowl with the water chestnuts. Chop the white part of the scallion and add to the shrimp.

ADDITIONAL PREPARATION
Combine the shrimp mixture with the salt, lightly beaten egg, pepper and 1 tablespoon corn oil.

Trim away the bread crusts and cut each bread slice in half diagonally to make 16 triangles. (I prefer Arnold or Pepperidge Farm bread.)

COOKING
Place the bread triangles on a cookie sheet in a 200 degree F. oven for 5 minutes, to dry. Spread the shrimp paste generously on each triangle. Sprinkle lightly with sesame seeds.

* SUBSTITUTION
If available, use fresh peeled water chestnuts instead of canned (see page 30).

Put about 2 inches of corn oil in a wok or pan and heat to 350 degrees F. Fry the Shrimp Toast until golden brown, first with the paste side down, then turned over, with the bread side down. Drain on paper towels before serving.

NOTE

You can freeze the shrimp paste, or freeze the Shrimp Toast before frying. Just make sure there is no moisture on them, because any liquid will make the hot fat spatter.

Deep-Fried Wontons
30 Wontons

If you can buy commercial wonton wrappers, this recipe is as easy as one-two-three. The wrappers come 60 to 80 in a package and keep well in the freezer, so you don't have to use them all at one time. But it isn't that difficult to make your own. Fried wontons are crisp, delicious, and inexpensive to make.

WRAPPERS

1 cup all-purpose flour	½ egg yolk
⅛ teaspoon baking soda	¼ cup water

FILLING

1 cup lean ground beef	¼ teaspoon white pepper
¼ cup chicken broth	1 tablespoon curry powder*
2 tablespoons soy sauce	1 tablespoon corn oil
1 teaspoon cornstarch	Corn oil for deep-frying

PROCESSING

Put the flour and baking soda in the work bowl with the steel blade. Beat the egg yolk lightly and add the

* SUBSTITUTION

Curry paste (I prefer Sun brand) is a delicious substitute for curry powder.

water. Turn the motor on and pour the liquid slowly through the feed tube until a ball of dough forms. Wrap the dough in aluminum foil and refrigerate at least 1 hour.

ADDITIONAL PREPARATON

Roll out the dough to a paper-thin sheet. Cut in 3-inch squares with a sharp knife. You should get about 30 wrappers.

For the filling, combine the ground beef, chicken broth, soy sauce, cornstarch, pepper, and curry powder. Mix well.

COOKING

Put 1 tablespoon of corn oil in a wok or pan over medium heat. Stir-fry the meat mixture until it is brown and cooked through. Cool.

To assemble, put 1 teaspoon of filling in the center of a wrapper, wet all the edges and fold in half. Press the wet edges firmly together to seal so the filling won't come out. Fold diagonally for triangular wontons, or squarely in half for rectangular wontons. (See illustration on page 31.)

Deep-fry in about 2 inches of corn oil at 250 degrees F. until golden brown. Drain on paper towels.

Serve with sweet-and-sour sauce and/or chutney.

NOTE

Deep-Fried Wontons can be frozen, then reheated in the oven.

Pan-Fried Wontons
36 Wontons

If you don't choose to make your own wrappers for this delicious snack, use commercial square egg-roll wrappers, cut in quarters.

WRAPPERS

2 cups all-purpose flour   ½ cup water
1 teaspoon salt

FILLING

3 scallions
¾ pound (1½ cups) lean   1 tablespoon corn oil
    ground beef
⅓ cup chicken broth   ½ teaspoon salt
2 tablespoons soy sauce   3 tablespoons corn oil
          2 tablespoons soy sauce
          2 tablespoons white vinegar

PROCESSING

With the steel blade in place, put flour and salt in the work bowl. Turn the motor on and pour the water gradually through the feed tube to make a smooth dough. Wrap the dough in aluminum foil and refrigerate at least 1 hour.

Cut the scallions into 1½-inch pieces and chop, using the steel blade.

ADDITIONAL PREPARATION

Roll out the dough to a thickness of 1/16 inch. Cut in 3-inch squares. This amount of dough should make about 36 wrappers.

For the filling, combine the scallions, beef, chicken broth, 2 tablespoons soy sauce, and 1 tablespoon corn oil. Put a heaping teaspoonful on one corner of a wrapper. Roll to the center to enclose the filling. Moisten the two facing corners, pinch together, and press tightly to seal. Continue until all wrappers are filled. (For one method of wrapping wontons, see sketches, page 31.)

COOKING

Bring 4 cups of water to a boil with the salt and 1 teaspoon of the corn oil. Drop in 10 to 15 wontons, or as many as will fit comfortably. Simmer for 3 minutes after the water returns to a boil. Remove with a slotted spoon to a wire rack. Repeat until all of the wontons are cooked and have cooled.

Set a flat-bottom Teflon pan on medium heat. Coat the bottom with oil and, when the pan is hot, put in as many wontons as will fit in a single layer. Pan-fry until one side is brown, then turn and brown the other side.

Mix the soy sauce and vinegar and serve with the fried wontons as a dip.

NOTE
Wontons can be frozen uncooked, or boiled and then frozen with just the pan-frying left for the last minute.

Spring Rolls
10 rolls

Spring Rolls are similar to egg rolls, but the wrapper is different. Spring-Roll wrappers are made from cooked dough. They become crisp when the rolls are deep-fried. As a teenager I was fascinated to watch the pastry chef making crepes for the Spring Rolls. He worked with a big piece of sticky dough, which he would smear on an ungreased griddle. When he pulled the dough up, there was just enough left on the griddle to make a paper-thin crepe. That took a lot of skill. During the last ten years these crepes have become available ready made in Chinese groceries in New York and other large cities. But I have developed a method very close to the pastry chef's, so you can try them at home.

WRAPPERS

2 cups flour	1 teaspoon corn oil
1 cup water	

You will also need:
A flat-bottom cast-iron pan
A new paintbrush about 4 inches wide

FILLING

1½ cups cabbage
6 medium-size fresh
  mushrooms
¼ cup bamboo shoots
½ pound lean pork or beef,
  partially frozen
2 tablespoons soy sauce

1 teaspoon cornstarch
2 scallions
3 tablespoons corn oil

1 egg, beaten
Corn oil for deep-frying

PROCESSING

Use the slicing disk to shred the cabbage and the mushrooms, the shredding disk for the bamboo shoots. Combine all three ingredients and set aside.

Cut the semifrozen meat into ¼-inch slices. Pack 4 slices at a time on edge in the feed tube with the slicing disk in place and process with pressure for uniform shreds. Mix the meat with the soy sauce and cornstarch. Cut the scallions in 1½-inch pieces and process with the steel blade to chop.

COOKING

To make the wrappers, mix the flour and water to a very smooth paste. Add a little extra water if needed. Set a flat-bottomed cast-iron pan over low heat. Put a few drops of corn oil on a paper towel and wipe the pan with it, leaving a very thin film of oil. Dip the paintbrush into the batter and paint the bottom of the pan with it. When the edges are dry, peel off the cooked crepe quickly with your fingers. The result is a paper-thin spring-roll wrapper. Stack on wax paper and repeat, regreasing the pan each time, until you have 10 wrappers. Or make more and freeze the extras.

Heat the 3 tablespoons corn oil in a wok or pan and stir-fry the cabbage, mushrooms, and bamboo shoots. Remove to a dish. Stir-fry the scallions and meat until the meat is thoroughly cooked and brown. Combine with the vegetables. Taste, and add more soy sauce if needed. Cool.

To assemble, put 2 tablespoons of filling in the lower part of each crepe. Roll once, fold the two sides toward the center, and roll again. Seal with beaten egg. (See sketch on page 32.)

Deep-fry Spring Rolls in two inches of corn oil, heated to 400 degrees F. When the rolls are golden brown and crisp, remove them from the oil and drain on paper towels.

Cut each roll in half and serve with plum sauce, chutney, or any dip you prefer.

NOTE
Spring Rolls can be frozen before or after drying.

Dumplings Northern Style
   30 dumplings

Ever since the Han Dynasty dumplings have been a favorite dish in the northern region of China. There are many ways to make dumplings, but the most popular is simply to boil them. Since they contain meat, a vegetable, and wheat flour, they really constitute a well-balanced meal in themselves.

WRAPPERS

½ teaspoon salt	⅓ cup water
1½ cups flour	

FILLING

1 package frozen chopped spinach	1 tablespoon corn oil
1 scallion	1 teaspoon salt
½ pound (1 cup) ground pork or beef	1 teaspoon corn oil
3½ tablespoons soy sauce	2 tablespoons soy sauce
2 tablespoon chicken broth	2 tablespoons white vinegar

PROCESSING
Put ½ teaspoon salt and 1¼ cups of flour in the work bowl with the steel blade in place. Turn the motor on and pour the water slowly through the feed tube.

Process until a ball of dough forms. Turn out on a board and knead in the rest of the flour until the dough is dry to the touch. Allow the dough to rest for 15 minutes.

ADDITIONAL PREPARATION

Defrost the spinach and squeeze out the liquid. Chop the scallion. By using the steel blade, combine the spinach and scallion with the ground meat, soy sauce, chicken broth, and corn oil.

Divide the dough into 30 little balls. Roll out each ball to a circle 2½ inches in diameter. Put 1 tablespoon of filling slightly below the center of each circle. Enclose the filling by folding up the bottom third of the wrapper, pleating, and sealing (See sketch on page 33.)

COOKING

Bring 2 quarts water and the salt and oil to a boil. (The oil will keep the dumplings from sticking together as they cook.) Put half the dumplings in the boiling water, return to a boil, and simmer 8 to 10 minutes. Lift out with a slotted spoon and drain on paper towels. Cook the remaining dumplings the same way.

Combine the soy sauce and vinegar and serve as a dip with the dumplings.

NOTE

Dumplings can be frozen before cooking and then cooked without defrosting. They can also be cooked, cooled, and then pan-fried.

Steamed Shrimp Dumplings
30 dumplings

These bite-size dumplings come from the southern region. The authentic wrapping is translucent because it uses wheat starch and tapioca flour. Since these ingredients are hard to find, I will first give you a recipe using easily available ingredients, and then the authentic version.

WRAPPERS
¾ cup flour   ⅓ cup boiling water
¼ cup cornstarch   1 tablespoon corn oil

FILLING
½ pound fresh shrimp,   ½ teaspoon salt
    cleaned and deveined   ½ teaspoon cornstarch
4 water chestnuts   ½ teaspoon dry sherry
1 scallion   1 tablespoon corn oil

PROCESSING
Put the dry ingredients in the work bowl with the steel blade in place. Mix the boiling water and oil and pour gradually through the tube, processing until a ball of dough forms. You may not need to use all the water, so add the last quarter cup gradually and stop as soon as the ball forms. Put the shrimp and the water chestnuts together in the work bowl with the steel blade and chop by turning the motor on and off 2 or 3 times. Be careful not to overprocess: you don't want a shrimp paste.

ADDITIONAL PREPARATION
Combine the filling ingredients and mix well.

Divide the dough into 30 little balls. Roll out each one to a paper-thin round. Place a teaspoon of the filling slightly below the center of the round, pleat the top two thirds, and enclose the filling by folding up the bottom third. (See sketch on page 33.) Moisten to seal.

COOKING
Put the dumplings on a greased heat-proof dish. Place the dish on a rack over boiling water in a steamer or covered pot. Steam over high heat for 8 minutes.

NOTE
Dumplings can be prepared ahead, frozen uncooked, and then steamed just before serving.

Authentic Version

WRAPPERS

¾ cup wheat starch (see page 30)
¼ cup tapioca flour (see page 30)

⅔ cup boiling water
1 tablespoon corn oil

Put the dry ingredients in the work bowl with the steel blade. Pour boiling water and oil gradually through the tube, processing until a ball of dough forms. Make dough rounds and fill as described above.

Scallion Pies
8 pies

It may surprise you that with the most basic, economical ingredients you can create such delectable crisp snacks. You will love them.

4 scallions
1½ cups flour
½ cup boiling water

1 tablespoon vegetable shortening
1 teaspoon salt
4 tablespoons corn oil

PROCESSNG

Cut the scallions in 1½-inch pieces. With the steel blade in place, put them in the work bowl and turn the motor on and off quickly two or three times to chop.

ADDITIONAL PREPARATION

Pour boiling water over the flour in a bowl and mix quickly. The dough will resemble cornmeal. Turn out onto a floured board, press together, then knead until smooth. Divide the dough in half.

Roll out half the dough into a rectangular sheet ⅛ inch thick. Rub half the shortening on the dough sheet. Sprinkle with half the scallions and half the salt. Roll tightly, like a jelly roll. Cut the roll into 4 pieces. Repeat with the other half of dough.

Roll piece of dough into a round shape, put between 2 layers of aluminum foil and roll out again, to about 4 inches in diameter. Repeat with the other seven scallion rolls. You will have 8 pies.

COOKING

Put ½ tablespoon corn oil into a frying pan with a cover. When the oil is hot, put in one pie. Cover the pan and brown over medium heat, first on one side, then the other. This should take only about a minute for each side. Keep pies warm in a low oven as you complete them. To serve, cut each pie into quarters.

NOTE

Scallion rolls can be frozen before cooking. When ready to serve, defrost, cut, roll out, and fry. Or freeze the completed pies, then reheat in a slow oven.

Sesame-Seed Puffs
24 puffs

These meatless snacks are delicious and, because you use a prepared dough for the wrappers, very easy to make.

2 bunches scallions	1 teaspoon salt
1 package frozen Pepperidge Farm patty shells, defrosted	1 egg
	⅓ cup white sesame seeds

PROCESSING

Chop scallions with the slicing disk by packing them together upright in the feed tube and using just enough pressure to keep them in contact with the blade.

ADDITIONAL PREPARATION

Cut each defrosted patty shell into quarters, form each quarter into a ball, and roll out into a circle about 2½ inches in diameter.

COOKING

Put chopped scallions into a Teflon pan over medium heat and cook, stirring, for one minute. Add salt and cool.

Place a teaspoonful of scallions in the center of each circle, fold in half and press the edges together. Brush with beaten egg. Sprinkle with sesame seeds. Bake in a 425 degree F. oven for 10 to 15 minutes, until golden brown.

NOTE

Freeze unbaked. To serve, defrost and bake as above.

Curry Crescents
24 crescents

I learned to make these when I was a teenager. One afternoon when we had relatives visiting, I made 200 crescents, and we finished them all. They are a great cocktail party "finger food."

WRAPPERS

1½ cups flour
½ teaspoon salt
½ teaspoon baking powder
1 tablespoon sugar
⅔ cup margarine or shortening, chilled
3 tablespoons ice water
½ beaten egg

FILLING

1 medium onion	1 tablespoon curry powder*
¼ pound (½ cup) lean ground beef	½ teaspoon sugar
	1 tablespoon corn oil
2 teaspoons soy sauce	
½ teaspoon cornstarch	½ beaten egg
⅛ teaspoon white pepper	

PROCESSING

To make the wrappers, put dry ingredients in the work bowl with the steel blade in place. Cut the shortening in cubes and add to the flour mixture. Process until the dough resembles cornmeal. Combine the ice water and half a beaten egg and pour slowly through the feed tube when the motor is on. Stop when the dough forms a ball, remove it, and wipe the work bowl.

Peel and quarter the onion and put it in the work bowl with the steel blade. Turn the motor on and off 2 or 3 times to chop.

ADDITIONAL PREPARATION

Mix the ground beef with the soy sauce, cornstarch, pepper, curry powder, and sugar.

Divide the dough into 24 pieces. Form each piece into a round ball, then flatten each ball to a 3-inch disk.

COOKING

Heat the corn oil in a wok or pan. Sauté the meat mixture until brown and cooked through. Remove to a bowl, using a slotted spoon. Put the chopped onions into the same pan and sauté until they are translucent but not brown. Add to the bowl with the meat, mix well, and allow to cool.

Put 1 teaspoon of filling in the center of each disk. Fold in half and flute the edges to seal the filling inside. (See sketch on page 33.) Brush with beaten egg and

* SUBSTITUTION

Sun-brand curry paste will give these crescents a more distinctive and authentic flavor.

prick with a fork so steam can escape. Arrange on a greased cookie sheet and bake in a 400 degree F. oven for 12 to 20 minutes.

NOTE
Curry Crescents can be frozen unbaked or baked.

Meat-Filled Steamed Buns
18 buns

These are the Chinese equivalent of American hamburgers. But the Chinese steam their breads instead of baking them, and these buns are cooked with the filling already inside.

WRAPPERS

2 cups flour

1 teaspoon salt

1 package dry yeast

1 tablespoon sugar

1 tablespoon warm water

½ cup warm water
   (110–115 degrees F.)

1 tablespoon corn oil

FILLING

1 scallion

4 ounces bamboo shoots

½ pound (1 cup) lean
   ground beef or pork

2 tablespoons soy sauce

¼ cup chicken broth

1 tablespoon corn oil

You will also need:
Wax paper, cut into 18 3-inch squares
An aluminum or bamboo steamer (see page 17)

PROCESSING
To make the wrappers, put the flour and salt in the work bowl with the steel blade in place. Mix the yeast, sugar, and warm water. Add the warm water and corn oil. Turn on the motor and process while pouring the liquid mixture through the feed tube in a steady stream. Turn off the motor when a ball of dough forms. Turn dough

out onto a floured board and knead until smooth, about 5 minutes.

Cut the scallion in 1½-inch pieces and put in the work bowl with the steel blade. Chop by turning the motor on and off once or twice. Remove to a bowl and then chop the bamboo shoots in the same way. Combine the scallion and bamboo shoots with the ground meat, soy sauce, chicken broth, and corn oil. Mix well.

ADDITIONAL PREPARATION

Divide the dough into 18 pieces. Form each piece into a ball, press flat and roll out into a 3-inch disk. Put 1 tablespoonful of filling in the center of each disk. Gather up the edges to the center and press together in little pleats to hold the filling. Put each bun on a square of wax paper with the smooth side up. Place on the steamer rack 1 inch apart and let rise until almost double in size, about 45 minutes to an hour.

COOKING

Steam buns over high heat for 12 minutes. Serve warm.

NOTE

Buns can be frozen after cooking. Cool, place on a cookie sheet to freeze, then pack in plastic bags. They can be reheated by steaming again. Or, with great success, in a microwave oven.

3
Salads

Chinese salads are really more like cold vegetables than traditional Western salads. And since they don't involve a lot of leafy greens that get soggy if left to sit around, you can prepare them way ahead. This leaves you more time to spend on other dishes that must be completed at the last minute. With one of these cold vegetable salads in the refrigerator, serving a balanced, healthful meal becomes easier, even on extra-busy days.

Broccoli Cold Mix
4 Servings

In my cooking classes the first lesson I teach is how to peel broccoli. Many of my students say they never know what to do with the broccoli stems, so they throw them away. But it is the stems that are important in Chinese cooking. (Actually, broccoli is the closest we can come in this country to a delicious Chinese vegetable with a long main stem, good and crunchy inside.) It takes a little patience to peel the broccoli stems, but the results are worth it. And your family probably won't even recognize what they are eating. (Save the flowerets for another dish—Beef and Broccoli, page 98, or Crunchy Broccoli, page 151.)

Stems from 2 bunches of fresh broccoli	**1 teaspoon vinegar**
3 tablespoons soy sauce	**2 tablespoons corn oil***
2 teaspoons sugar	**2 teaspoons salt**

PREPARATION

Starting from the root end, peel off the tough outer fibers of the broccoli stems. A plain paring knife works better for this than a swivel-type peeler. When you have removed all of the stringy white fibers, roll-cut the stems into triangular pieces. (See roll-cut sketch on page 32.) Cut the smaller pieces into matching triangles.

Combine the soy sauce, sugar, vinegar, and oil in a small dish and set aside.

COOKING

Bring 4 cups water to a boil in a saucepan with 2 teaspoons salt. Add the cut stems. When they turn a darker green and the water starts to boil again (usually in less than a minute), transfer them to a strainer, using a slotted spoon. Run cold water over them for a few seconds, then drain and store in the refrigerator.

To serve, combine the broccoli stems with the sauce.

You can keep the blanched stems in the refrigerator for up to a day, but freezing is not recommended.

* SUBSTITUTION
If sesame-seed oil is available, it will make a flavorful sauce.

Asparagus Cold Mix
4 Servings

When asparagus is in season, I can eat it every day. Since I like it so much, I find all sorts of ways to prepare it. This method is almost identical to the Broccoli Cold Mix (page 50), but the cutting is a little different.

1 pound fresh asparagus stalks	1 teaspoon vinegar
3 tablespoons soy sauce	2 tablespoons corn oil*
1 teaspoon sugar	2 teaspoons salt

PREPARATION

There are two ways to cut asparagus. You can simply wash it, discard the white parts, and cut the green stalks diagonally at a 45-degree angle into ¼-inch slices. Or use a swivel-type vegetable peeler to remove the little green scales and the outer skin, then cut the stalks straight across into 2-inch-long pieces.

Combine the soy sauce, sugar, vinegar, and corn oil in a small dish and set aside.

COOKING

Bring 4 cups of water to a boil in a saucepan with 2 teaspoons salt. Drop in the asparagus pieces. As soon as they turn a darker green (usually in less than a minute) lift them out with a slotted spoon and transfer them to a strainer. Run cold tap water over the asparagus, drain, and store in the refrigerator.

Serve the asparagus the same day you prepare it. Keeping the pieces in the refrigerator too long will make them soggy. When ready to serve, combine with the sauce and toss lightly.

* SUBSTITUTION
If sesame-seed oil is available, it will make a flavorful sauce.

Cucumber Fans
4 Servings

Since this recipe needs a few hours of soaking time, I always make enough for more than one meal. The flavor gets stronger as the days go by. If you don't like spicy food, you can omit the red pepper and Tabasco sauce. The fancy cutting makes the dish more interesting, but it is optional; you can simply slice the cucumbers instead.

4 large cucumbers	2 tablespoons corn oil*
1 tablespoon salt	1 tablespoon crushed red
3 tablespoons soy sauce	peppers (optional)
3 cloves garlic, chopped	1 teaspoon Tabasco sauce
2 teaspoons sugar	(optional)
1 tablespoon vinegar	

PREPARATION

Cut off both tips of the cucumbers, cut them lengthwise in quarters, and remove the seeds. Cut each long piece into 2-inch lengths. Make 5 lengthwise slits in each piece, three quarters of the way down, being careful not to cut through to the bottom. Press with a knife blade to get a fanlike effect. When all the pieces have been cut, place them in a bowl and mix in the salt. Let stand at room temperature for 2 to 3 hours. Drain off the liquid that accumulates, rinse the cucumber fans under cold water, and drain.

Combine the rest of the ingredients and mix well with the cucumber fans. Let stand at least three hours before serving to develop the flavors. This dish can be kept in the refrigerator for a week.

* **SUBSTITUTION**
If sesame-seed oil is available, it will make a flavorful sauce.

Celery Shreds
4 Servings

This is a very pretty salad. The dressing is a little different, as it is thick and contains a surprise ingredient—peanut butter. You can make it as spicy as you like or skip the Tabasco sauce completely.

1 large celery plant	½ teaspoon Tabasco sauce
1 large carrot	(optional)
2 tablespoons peanut butter	2 teaspoons sugar
2 tablespoons soy sauce	½ teaspoon mustard
1 tablespoon wine vinegar	

PROCESSING

Wash the celery and remove the stringy fibers. Cut the stalks into 2-inch-long pieces. With the shredding disk of the processor in place, lay the celery pieces lengthwise one on top of the other in the feed tube. Process with firm pressure to get long shreds. Repeat until all of the stalks have been shredded. Put the celery in a colander and set aside.

Scrape the carrot and cut it into 2-inch-long pieces. Lay the pieces lengthwise one on top of the other in the feed tube. Process with light pressure for long carrot shreds.

ADDITIONAL PREPARTION

Put the peanut butter in a small bowl and gradually stir in the soy sauce and vinegar to make a smooth sauce. Add the Tabasco, sugar, and mustard, and set aside.

COOKING

Bring four cups of water to a boil. Run the boiling water over the celery in the colander. Quickly rinse celery under cold tap water, drain, and place in a large bowl. Add the carrot shreds. Just before serving, pour the sauce over the vegetables and toss.

Authentic Version

Use 2 tablespoons sesame-seed paste instead of the peanut butter and ½ teaspoon hot chili oil instead of the Tabasco sauce. (See page 28.)

Bean-Sprout Toss
4 Servings

Bean sprouts are much more nourishing than the beans themselves. Many varieties of beans can be used; I prefer mung beans, which are tender and tasty. It is easy to grow your own—I tell you how in the Vegetable section, on page 155. It's fun, and the quality and freshness are superior to bean sprouts you buy in the store.

1 pound mung-bean sprouts	1 teaspoon corn oil*
2 tablespoons soy sauce	2 tablespoons white sesame
1 teaspoon sugar	seeds
½ teaspoon vinegar	

PREPARATION
Remove the stringy tails from the bean sprouts. This step is optional, but if you take the time to do this, it will improve the flavor of the salad. Place the sprouts in a strainer.

Combine the soy sauce, sugar, vinegar, and corn oil, and set aside.

COOKING
Bring 4 cups water to a boil and pour over the bean sprouts. Quickly run the sprouts under cold tap water and drain. Mix well with the sauce. Serve, sprinkled with sesame seeds, in individual salad bowls. Make this

*SUBSTITUTION
If sesame-seed oil is available, it will make a flavorful dressing. For a hotter version, use sesame-seed oil with chili instead. (See page 29.)

salad as close to serving time as possible; it does not keep well.

Radish Flowers
4 Servings

You must plan ahead to serve this salad because it requires several hours of soaking. Yet there is very little actual work involved, especially if you have the special radish cutter called a radish rosette. This is a very pretty salad.

2 large cucumbers	½ cup white vinegar
1 package red radishes	¼ cup sugar
4 tablespoons salt	

PROCESSING

Peel the cucumbers, cut in lengthwise quarters and remove the seeds. Cut each quarter into 2-inch pieces. With the shredding disk in place, pack the feed tube with cucumber pieces laid sideways, one on top of the other. Process with pressure to get nice long cucumber shreds. Combine with 1½ tablespoons of salt and set aside.

ADDITIONAL PREPARATION

Wash and stem the radishes. Make flowers with the radish cutter. Or cut petals by hand with a sharp knife, by making four thin slices around the circumference of the radish from top to bottom. (Be careful not to cut all the way through.) Mix radishes with the remaining 2½ tablespoons salt. Allow the cucumber shreds and the radishes to stand in separate bowls for 2 to 3 hours.

Rinse the radishes in cool water and drain. Combine the vinegar and sugar. Reserve 2 tablespoons of the mixture, pour the rest over the radishes, and allow to soak for 2 hours. Pour off the accumulated cucumber liquid and mix the reserved two tablespoons of vinegar and sugar with the cucumber shreds. To serve, put a bed of cucumber shreds on each plate and top with three or four Radish Flowers.

Chopped Spinach Salad
4 Servings

This recipe from the eastern region of China pleases everyone, but it is particularly suitable for vegetarian diets.

1 can (8 ounces) water chestnuts	2 pounds fresh spinach
4 ounces fresh mushrooms*	3 tablespoons soy sauce
3 tablespoons corn oil*	2 teaspoons sugar

PROCESSING

The mushrooms and water chestnuts should be cooked slightly before processing. Put water chestnuts in a saucepan with the liquid from the can. Bring to a boil, then drain and cool. Wash the mushrooms and pat dry with paper towels. Heat corn oil in a wok or frying pan. Put in the mushrooms and sauté for a minute or two. Remove from heat. Drain the mushrooms and reserve the oil.

With the steel blade in place, put the water chestnuts in the work bowl and chop coarsely by turning the motor on and off 2 or 3 times. Remove the water chestnuts to a bowl and chop the mushrooms coarsely in the same manner. Mix the water chestnuts and mushrooms together and set aside.

* SUBSTITUTIONS

Chinese black mushrooms (see page 26) and sesame-seed oil are flavorful substitutes for the fresh mushrooms and the corn oil. One ounce of the dried mushrooms is the equivalent of 4 ounces of fresh mushrooms.

COOKING

Wash the spinach thoroughly. Bring 4 quarts of water to a boil and drop in the spinach. Cook just until the leaves are wilted, then pour off the water. Use cheese-cloth or clean dish towels to squeeze out the remaining moisture. Cool. Chop the spinach lightly and combine in a large bowl with the water chestnuts and mushrooms.

When ready to serve, mix the oil in which the mushrooms were sautéed with the soy sauce and sugar and pour over the chopped vegetables. This dish can be kept in the refrigerator for a day or two.

Pickled Cabbage
4 to 6 Servings

It takes about 3 days to pickle the cabbage, but there is no last-minute work at all. This is a crunchy and appetizing salad.

2 pounds cabbage	⅛ teaspoon ginger powder
3 tablespoons salt	1 tablespoon crushed red
4 cups water	peppers (optional)
2 tablespoons dry gin	

PREPARATION

Wash and core the cabbage and cut into pieces about 2 inches square. Add the salt to the water. Heat slightly if necessary to dissolve completely. Cool. Add gin, ginger, and red peppers. Pack the cabbage pieces tightly in a large jar. Pour in enough liquid to cover and close the lid tightly. Store in the refrigerator for at least 3 days. Serve the cabbage without the liquid. Pickled Cabbage will keep for 2 weeks, refrigerated in its liquid.

Sweet-and-Sour Cauliflower
4 Servings

This is an easy salad, but it does take 2 days for the cauliflower to absorb the flavors of the marinade.

1 carrot	1 cup white vinegar
1 small cauliflower	1 tablespoon salt
½ cup sugar	

PROCESSING
Scrape the carrot and cut in 2-inch lengths to fit the feed tube. Use the slicing disk and light pressure to get uniform thin slices.

ADDITIONAL PREPARATION
Cut away the outer leaves and hard core of the cauliflower, and break into flowerets. Dissolve sugar in vinegar and set aside.

COOKING
Bring 6 cups of water to boil with the salt. Put in the cauliflower and cook just until the water returns to a boil. Lift out cauliflower and drain well on paper towels. Cool. Combine with the carrot slices and spoon into a large jar. Pour over the sugar-vinegar solution, cover, and refrigerate for at least 2 days before serving. Sweet-and-sour Cauliflower will keep, refrigerated, for up to a week.

4
Soups

Hot soup can really warm you up on a chilly day. In Chinese cooking, there is no set rule for serving soup; it can be a first course, or come between courses or at the end of a banquet. A hearty soup served with a selection of hot snacks (see Chapter 1) can be a delicious meal in itself. All these simple and tasty soups call for a basic stock to start with. If you do not have the time to make your own, you can use chicken-bouillon cubes dissolved in water, or canned chicken broth, but homemade stock is more flavorful and nourishing. If you save chicken bones and carcasses from other recipes and keep them in the freezer until you have the required amount, homemade stock is also very economical.

A word about seasoning! I find the soups served in most restaurants too salty. My recipes are lightly seasoned, but you can add more salt and pepper to your family's taste.

The Basic Stock

Chinese chefs usually make their own stock because they feel it improves the flavor of any dish. In fact, a good stock can be the secret of good cooking.

4 cups cut-up chicken, or 1 whole 3-pound chicken, or 4 pounds chicken bones	6 cups cold water 1 scallion 2 tablespoons dry vermouth Salt and pepper to taste

COOKING

Fill a large saucepan with water. Bring it to a boil and drop in the chicken or bones. When the water returns to a boil, pour it off, rinse the chicken, and wash the pot. Return the chicken to the pot with 6 cups of water and bring to a boil. Add the scallion and vermouth and simmer for at least 2 hours. Season with salt and pepper to taste and simmer another hour.

Cool, strain the stock into jars and refrigerate. Remove the fat that will rise to the top after it has solidified. Stock will keep a week in the refrigerator. You can also freeze it in plastic containers.

Tomato and Egg-Drop Soup
4 Servings

This delicious soup is not only easy to make, it is also very pretty with its yellow, orange, and green colors.

2 tomatoes*	2 scallions*
1 egg	3 cups chicken stock

* SUBSTITUTIONS

Turn this into seaweed egg-drop soup by substituting 2 sheets of dried seaweed (see page 27), cut into small pieces, for the tomatoes. Add them before the egg. Garnish with coriander (see page 27) instead of the scallions.

PREPARATION

Cut the tomatoes in ¼-inch slices. Beat the egg. Chop the green parts of the scallions. (Reserve the whites for another dish.)

COOKING

Bring the chicken stock to a boil and add the tomato slices. When the stock returns to a boil, turn the heat down low to simmer. Pour beaten egg in a thin stream into the soup. Remove from the heat and pour into serving dishes. Garnish with the scallion greens.

Chicken and Corn Soup
6 to 8 Servings

This is one of my favorites, hearty enough for a luncheon main dish but tasty enough for a banquet course. It is one of the stars of southern Chinese cuisine.

1 medium-size chicken breast	1 ounce Virginia ham*
2 egg whites	4 tablespoons cornstarch
1 can (16 ounces) cream-style corn	6 tablespoons water
	6 cups chicken stock
	½ teaspoon salt

PROCESSING

Remove bones and tendons from the chicken breast and cut it in 2-inch-square pieces. Beat one of the egg whites until foamy but not stiff. With the steel blade in place, put the chicken pieces in the work bowl. Turn the motor on and off quickly to mince the chicken. Add one beaten egg white and the corn and process 3 seconds. Remove and set aside. Rinse and dry the work bowl, replace the steel blade, and mince the ham.

* SUBSTITUTION

Cooked Smithfield ham gives a distinctive flavor and is the closest in character to Chinese ham.

ADDITIONAL PREPARATION

Mix the cornstarch and water. Beat the second egg white until foamy.

COOKING

Bring the chicken stock to a boil, add salt, and stir in the chicken mixture. Bring to a boil again, then lower heat to simmer. Stir the cornstarch-and-water mixture and add it gradually to the soup to thicken it. Simmer for 1 more minute, then pour the second egg white very slowly into the soup. Stir gently. To serve, pour into a soup tureen and garnish with minced ham.

NOTE

Reheating will not change the flavor of this soup, so you can make it a day in advance. You can also freeze portions in small plastic containers for quick snacks. Garnish with ham just before serving.

Hot and Sour Soup
4 to 6 Servings

Hot and Sour Soup has introduced many Americans to the spicy cuisine of western China. Here are two versions, one made with readily available ingredients and the other an authentic version using some of the more unusual Chinese ingredients, like tree ears and tiger-lilly buds.

⅓ cup lean pork, partially
　frozen
⅓ cup bamboo shoots
1 teaspoon soy sauce
2½ tablespoons cornstarch
1 scallion
1 egg
2 tablespoons water
2 tablespoons corn oil

4 cups chicken broth
⅓ cup canned sliced
　mushrooms*
2 tablespoons white vinegar
1 teaspoon salt
½ teaspoon white pepper
1 tablespoon Tobasco
　sauce*

PROCESSING

With a sharp knife, slice pork ⅛-inch thick across the grain. Stack 4 or 5 slices on end in the feed tube and shred with the slicing disk. Put the shredding disk in place and shred the bamboo shoots.

ADDITIONAL PREPARATION

Mix the pork with the soy sauce and ½ teaspoon cornstarch. Slice the scallion. Beat the egg. Combine the remaining cornstarch with the water.

COOKING

Heat corn oil in a large saucepan. Stir-fry the pork until it is fully cooked. Add the chicken broth, bamboo shoots, and mushrooms and bring to a boil. Add vinegar, salt, pepper, and Tabasco sauce. Stir the cornstarch mixture and add gradually to the soup to thicken it. Simmer 1 minute, then pour the beaten egg in a thin stream into the simmering soup. The egg will set in little strands. Remove from heat, pour into bowls, and serve, garnished with scallions.

* SUBSTITUTIONS

Instead of the canned mushrooms and Tabasco sauce, use 4 or 5 Chinese black mushrooms, soaked for an hour to reconstitute, and 1 tablespoonful hot oil (see pages 27, 28) for a more authentic flavor.

Authentic Version

In addition to substituting Chinese black mushrooms and hot oil, the following ingredients (see Glossary) should be added:

⅓ cup tree ears
10 to 12 tiger-lily buds
1 cake soft bean curd

Cover the mushrooms, ears, and tiger-lily buds with boiling water and soak for half an hour. Remove the mushroom stems, pick over the tree ears to remove any bits of wood, and cut the lily buds in half. Slice the bean curd. Add all these ingredients with the bamboo shoots. Add the hot oil with the vinegar. For an even hotter flavor, add 1 tablespoon sesame-seed oil with chili (see page 29) before serving.

Chicken and Ham Soup
4 Servings

This is a clear soup from the eastern region. The red ham, yellow egg, and white chicken make it very attractive, and it is a wonderful way to utilize leftover ham and chicken from holiday dinners.

½ cooked chicken breast
2 ounces Virginia ham or
    baked ham
½ cup bamboo shoots

1 egg
4 cups chicken stock
Salt and pepper to taste

PROCESSING
Shred chicken, ham, and bamboo shoots.

COOKING
Lightly grease a frying pan and set over medium heat. Beat the egg and pour into the pan, rotating to cover the pan and make a thin egg crepe. Cook until the

egg is set. Remove from the pan and cool. Roll the crepe and slice it thin to make shreds.

Bring the chicken stock to a boil. Add the shredded chicken, ham, and bamboo shoots. Add salt and pepper to taste. When the soup returns to a boil, pour into a serving dish and garnish with the egg shreds.

Spinach and Fish-Ball Soup
4 to 6 Servings

This is a classic recipe from the eastern region, where it was always considered a special treat because it was such a time-consuming job to make the fish balls. Now, of course, the electric food processor makes it easy. The dish is still considered very special, though, partly because of the taste—delicious!—and partly because of the ancient symbolism connected with it. The green spinach and the white fish balls represent the two finest jade colors. To carry out the symbolism, allow only two fish balls for each serving, because perfect white jade is hard to come by.

¾ cup fish fillet (flounder, haddock, yellow pike, sole)
2 egg whites, slightly beaten
¼ teaspoon salt
⅛ teaspoon white pepper
2 tablespoons chicken broth
¼ teaspoon salt
Corn oil for dipping
4 cups chicken stock
4 ounces fresh spinach, washed and drained

PROCESSING

Remove any bones from the fish, cut into 2-inch pieces, and put in the work bowl of the food processor with the steel blade in place. Process the fish until smooth. Add the egg whites, salt and pepper, and process again. Pour chicken broth through the feed tube while the machine is running and process again until a very smooth paste forms.

COOKING

Bring 4 cups of water to a boil in a saucepan with ½ teaspoon salt. Lower heat just to the simmering point. To form the fish balls, dip a teaspoon in corn oil, then scoop up some fish paste and form a ball with the spoon and your fingers. As you make each ball, drop it into the water. Dip the spoon in oil each time to keep the fish paste from sticking. The fish balls will float to the surface when they are done. As they pop up, remove them with a slotted spoon and transfer them to cold water.

Bring the chicken stock to a boil, add the spinach, and cook one minute. Add the fish balls. When the soup comes to a boil again, it is ready to serve.

The Grand Soup
8 to 10 Servings

This tasty soup is so rich that, by simply adding some noodles, you can serve it as a complete meal. Since it requires lengthy cooking, a crock pot would be ideal, but in order to use even a large crock pot, you will have to cut the recipe in half to fit everything in.

1 Chinese celery or Napa cabbage (see Glossary)	½ fresh ham, preferably the shank end
2 scallions	1 ham bone*
1 chicken, 3 pounds or more	Salt and pepper to taste
	2 tablespoons vermouth

PREPARATION

Wash the cabbage and cut in 8 pieces. Cut the scallions into 1-inch pieces.

* SUBSTITUTION

A Smithfield ham bone will give an even better flavor. The slow cooking releases all the flavor from the bone.

COOKING

Half-fill a large Dutch oven or spaghetti pot with water and bring it to a boil. Put in the chicken, ham, and ham bone, bring to a second boil, and pour off the water. Wash the pot. Return the chicken, ham, and bone to the pot, cover with water, and bring to a boil. Add the scallions and salt and pepper to taste. Simmer for 3 hours. Put in the cabbage and simmer another hour.

NOTE

You can bring the whole pot to the dining table and let each person choose what he likes, or portion it out beforehand. This soup can be made ahead and reheated.

Chinese Fish Chowder
4 Servings

This is another popular soup from the eastern region, where there are long seacoasts and many lakes, and plentiful fish.

1 whole fish, 1 to 1¼ pounds (whiting, bass or yellow pike)	3 tablespoons water
	3 cups chicken stock
	1 tablespoon dry vermouth
1 scallion	⅛ teaspoon salt
2 garlic cloves	⅛ teaspoon white pepper
2 tablespoons cornstarch	¼ cup bamboo shoots

PREPARATION

Clean the fish thoroughly. Chop the scallion. Mix the cornstarch with the water in a small dish.

COOKING

Put the fish in a pot, cut in half if necessary, and add ½ cup of the chicken stock, the vermouth, and salt and pepper. Bring to a boil and reduce heat. Simmer, covered, for 5 minutes. Allow to cool with the cover on.

When the fish is cool, remove all bones and skin.

Put the fish in a bowl and strain over it the liquid from the pot.

Bring the rest of the chicken stock to a boil and add the bamboo shoots and fish. When it boils again, thicken the soup with the cornstarch mixture. Simmer for 1 minute, pour into bowls, and serve garnished with the chopped scallion.

NOTE
To save time, the fish can be cooked and boned in advance and kept in the refrigerator for a day or so.

Authentic Version

Substitute Chinese coriander for the scallion and add a cake of soft bean curd, cut in small pieces, with the fish.

Mock-Melon Soup
4 Servings

Chinese winter melon is a large squash resembling a round watermelon. In Cantonese cuisine a hollowed winter melon, filled with diced meat and seasonings and steamed for 8 to 10 hours, is a gourmet's delight sometimes served at banquet dinners. A skilled chef might even show off by carving dragons and other designs on the skin of the melon. I have found that cooked cucumber resembles winter melon in appearance and texture, so you can enjoy this delicious soup even when winter melon is unavailable.

2 large cucumbers*	2 tablespoons cornstarch
½ chicken breast	3 tablespoons water
½ ounce baked ham*	3 cups chicken stock

PROCESSING
Peel the cucumbers, cut in half lengthwise, and scoop out the seeds with a teaspoon. With the slicing disk in place, pack the feed tube with pieces of cucumber cut to fit standing up. Process with pressure for neat, crescent-shaped slices.

Cut the chicken breast in 2-inch pieces and put in the work bowl with the steel blade in place. Mince by turning the motor on and off quickly a few times. Check to make sure you are not overprocessing. Wash the work bowl and the steel blade, then mince the ham. Set the ham aside to use as a garnish.

ADDITIONAL PREPARATION
Mix the cornstarch with water in a small dish.

COOKING
Put the cucumbers in a saucepan with water to cover. Cook, covered, for 5 minutes, or until cucumbers are translucent. Pour off the water and add chicken stock. Bring to a boil, stir in the minced chicken, and lower heat to simmer. Stir in the cornstarch mixture gradually to thicken the soup and simmer 1 more minute. Pour into bowls and garnish with the minced ham.

NOTE
This soup can be made in advance and reheated without changing the texture of the cucumbers.

* SUBSTITUTIONS
If winter melon is available, substitute 1½ pounds for the cucumbers. The flavor of Smithfield ham is superior.

Crabmeat and Mushroom Soup
4 Servings

When fresh crabs are in season, it is a treat to serve this delicious soup. Steam the crabs first, then use the meat. Frozen crabmeat is a satisfactory substitute, but canned crabmeat is not as good.

1 cup fresh mushrooms	1 tablespoon dry vermouth
2 tablespoons cornstarch	3 cups chicken stock
3 tablespoons water	1 tablespoon soy sauce
1 tablespoon corn oil	(optional)
½ package frozen Alaskan king crabmeat, defrosted*	

PROCESSING
With the slicing disk in place, pack the feed tube with mushrooms and process with pressure to get neat slices.

ADDITIONAL PREPARATION
Mix the cornstarch with water in a small dish.

COOKING
Heat oil in a large saucepan and sauté the mushrooms until they are soft, about 1 minute. Add the crabmeat and vermouth, cover and heat until you see steam escaping from the pot. Put in the chicken stock, bring to a boil, and reduce the heat. Thicken the soup with the cornstarch mixture and simmer 1 more minute. Add soy sauce and serve.

* SUBSTITUTION
When available, use a cup of fresh Maryland crabmeat instead of the frozen.

Watercress Soup
  4 Servings

The Cantonese love watercress; they believe that it cools the internal system of the body. This is the most popular of all home-cooked soups.

1 bunch watercress	½ teaspoon cornstarch
½ cup cooked lean pork or cooked chicken	⅛ teaspoon white pepper
1 teaspoon soy sauce	4 cups chicken broth or stock

PREPARATION
Wash the watercress. Cut the pork or chicken into slices about ⅛ inch thick and 2 inches square. Combine meat with the soy sauce, cornstarch, and pepper.

COOKING
Bring the chicken broth to a boil. Add the watercress and marinated meat, and return to a boil. Lower heat, simmer for 10 minutes and serve.

Wonton Soup
  4 Servings

In China wontons are served as a snack in broth rather than as a soup course. If you want to do the same, you should allow about 10 wontons per person. When you serve wonton soup as a first course, two wontons per person will be sufficient because they are quite filling. It is not hard to make your own wontons, especially if you buy commercially prepared wrappers. Make the wontons ahead and freeze them, uncooked, in plastic bags. When you want to use them, simply take out as many as you need and drop them, still frozen, in boiling water to cook. Following this recipe you will find complete directions for making wontons. Here is how to use them in a delicious soup.

| 8 wontons, frozen (recipe follows) | 1 cup fresh spinach, washed* |
| 3 cups chicken stock | 1 slice baked ham, cut in quarters* |

COOKING

Bring 2 cups of water to a boil, add the frozen wontons, return to a boil, and simmer for 2 or 3 minutes. Remove the wontons to a plate and discard the water. Bring the chicken stock to a boil, add the spinach, and cook until wilted, about ½ minute. Add the wontons and heat through.

Put 2 wontons and some spinach in each bowl, pour in broth and garnish with a ham slice.

How to Make and Freeze Wontons
30 to 36 Wontons

WRAPPERS

Commercial wonton wrappers are convenient to use and keep well in the freezer. But if you would like to make your own, this is how to do it.

2 cups flour
½ teaspoon salt
1 egg
½ cup warm water
Additional flour for
    kneading

PROCESSING

Put the flour and salt in the work bowl with the steel blade. Beat the egg with the water. Turn on the mo-

* SUBSTITUTIONS

The green outer leaves of bok choy are a good substitute for spinach. Use any ham you prefer. If Smithfield ham is available, it gives more flavor, but the main purpose of the ham in this soup is to add a touch of color.

tor and gradually pour the egg mixture through the tube. Continue processing until a ball of dough forms. Turn the dough out on a floured board and knead, adding more flour bit by bit until the dough is dry to the touch. Wrap in aluminum foil and refrigerate for at leat an hour.

ADDITIONAL PREPARATION

Roll out the dough to $\frac{1}{16}$ inch or even thinner and cut in 3-inch squares. To get as many squares as possible, maintain a rectangular shape when you roll the dough. Do not try to combine the odd pieces to form new ones.

FILLING

2 scallions
½ pound (1 cup) ground
   lean pork, beef
   or chicken
¼ cup chicken broth

3 tablespoons soy sauce
½ package frozen chopped
   spinach, defrosted*
1 tablespoon corn oil

PROCESSING

Cut the scallions in 1½-inch pieces. Put in the work bowl with the steel blade and chop.

If the meat has not been ground by the butcher, you can do it yourself with the food processor. Cut meat in 1½-inch cubes and partially freeze. Process with the steel blade, turning the motor on and off quickly until the meat is coarsely ground.

ADDITIONAL PREPARATION

Combine the chicken broth, soy sauce, and meat. Mix in the spinach and oil to form a smooth pastelike filling.

* SUBSTITUTION

Celery cabbage, Napa cabbage, and bok choy are all good substitutes for the spinach. Cook them in a little water until soft, chop coarsely, squeeze out the liquid, and use as directed for spinach.

ASSEMBLY

There are many ways to wrap wontons. These are the easiest. (See page 31.)

1. Put a scant teaspoon of the filling in the center of the wrapper, moisten the edges with water, and fold in half.

2. Put ½ teaspoon of filling at the tip of one corner. Roll up to the center. Moisten the facing corners with water and press to seal. The fourth corner remains unsealed, but this wrapping keeps the filling firmly inside.

NOTE

As you finish assembling the wontons, line them up on a cookie sheet. Freeze, then remove from the sheet and store in plastic bags. Wontons will keep for up to 3 months in the freezer.

5
Chicken Main Dishes

Steamed Chicken—Basic Recipe

Steamed Chicken is delicious served with its own natural juices or as the starting point for more elaborate recipes, which follow. Once you master this easy technique, you will probably invent your own variations. If you have a large pot, a turkey roaster, or a wok, plus a rack and an ovenproof bowl, you are in business. Just remember to allow 2 days for the chicken to "season" before cooking.

1 roasting chicken, 3½ to 4 pounds	½ teaspoon white pepper
	2 scallions
2½ tablespoons coarse salt (preferably), or regular salt	1 tablespoon cornstarch
	2 tablespoons water

PREPARATION
Wash the chicken thoroughly, making sure all of the intestinal parts have been removed. Pat dry. Combine the salt and pepper and rub the chicken with the mixture,

inside and out. Place the chicken in a plastic food bag, tightly closed, and leave in the refrigerator for 2 days.

Slice the scallions, keeping the white and green parts separate.

COOKING

When ready to cook the chicken, remove it from the plastic bag, put the scallion whites in the cavity and place the chicken in a ceramic or glass heat-proof bowl large enough to hold it comfortably. Set the bowl on a rack in a large pot holding 2 inches of water. Steam, covered, over high heat for 45 minutes. Check the water level occasionally and add more boiling water as it evaporates.

Turn off the heat and let the chicken cool in the pot until you can handle it. By this time juices from the chicken will have collected in the bowl. Move the chicken to another bowl (where more juices will collect) and, with a boning knife or any knife you are comfortable with, bone the chicken. Skilled chefs can do this and leave the chicken intact. Since you are going to cut the chicken up anyway, it isn't necessary to do this. But don't just hack away; you want nicely shaped serving pieces. Arrange the chicken on a serving dish.

Skim the fat off the collected juices and then bring them to a boil. Combine the cornstarch with water and pour it gradually into the boiling liquid, stopping when you reach the consistency you like. Pour over the chicken, garnish with chopped scallion greens, and serve.

NOTE

Cooked chicken can be wrapped in foil or enclosed in a plastic bag and stored up to 2 days in the refrigerator. Put the liquid from the chicken into a jar and refrigerate. You can also freeze the salted chicken before cooking, or the cooked chicken.

Steamed Chicken with Scallion Sauce
4 Servings

4 scallions
1 steamed chicken, cut in
  pieces (recipe on
  page 76)
1 teaspoon cornstarch
½ cup plus 1 tablespoon
  water
2 tablespoons corn oil

¼ cup soy sauce
½ cup chicken broth or
  liquid from steamed
  chicken
½ cup water
½ teaspoon sugar
½ teaspoon ginger powder*

PROCESSING
Cut the scallions into 1½-inch pieces and put in the work bowl with the steel blade. Chop by turning the motor on and off 2 or 3 times.

ADDITIONAL PREPARATION
Arrange the chicken pieces on a serving platter, cover with foil and keep warm in a very low oven while you prepare the sauce.

Mix cornstarch with 1 tablespoon water.

COOKING
Heat the corn oil in a saucepan. When the oil is hot, add the chopped scallions and cook over medium heat until brown. Add the soy sauce, chicken broth, ½ cup water, sugar, and ginger, and bring to a boil. Stir in the cornstarch mixture slowly and cook, stirring, for 30 seconds. Pour the sauce over the chicken and serve.

Steamed Chicken with Ham and Broccoli
4 Servings

In southern China, where this dish is a favorite, it is

* SUBSTITUTION
If fresh ginger root is available, substitute 1 tablespoon finely minced root for the powder.

called by name which means "jade-tree chicken" because the green broccoli represents the finest color of jade.

1 whole steamed chicken, or 2 large chicken breasts prepared the same way (recipe on page 76)	1 bunch broccoli
	2 teaspoons cornstarch
	2 tablespoons water
	1 teaspoon salt
¼ pound sliced Virginia ham or any baked or boiled ham*	1 cup liquid from steamed chicken, diluted with water

PREPARATION

Bone chicken and cut into pieces approximately 2 inches by ¾ inch by ¾ inch. Cut the ham slices into pieces approximately 2 inches by ¾ inch. Arrange the chicken and ham alternately on a serving platter with the pieces overlapping. Cover with foil and keep warm in a low oven.

Cut the broccoli head into individual flowers. Reserve the stems for another use (for example, Broccoli Cold Mix, on page 50).

Combine the cornstarch and water and set aside.

COOKING

Bring 4 cups of water to a boil and add 1 teaspoon salt. Blanch the broccoli just until the water boils again. Transfer to a colander and run under cold water from the tap to cool and stop cooking. Pat the flowerets dry with paper towels and arrange them on the platter with the chicken and ham.

Skim off the fat, then heat the liquid from the steamed chicken. Add water to make 1 cup of liquid. Taste and see whether it needs more diluting or more salt. Bring to a boil and stir in the cornstarch mixture gradu-

---

* SUBSTITUTION
Smithfield ham, which is more salty and resembles Chinese ham, will give the dish added flavor.

ally to thicken. Pour over the chicken, ham, and broccoli and serve.

Steamed Chicken with Hot Sauce
4 Servings

1 steamed chicken (recipe on page 76)	2 tablespoons soy sauce
3 garlic cloves	¼ cup liquid from steamed chicken
3 tablespoons corn oil	1 tablespoon Tabasco sauce
2 tablespoons crushed red pepper	

PREPARATION

Bone the chicken and cut into serving pieces. Arrange on a serving platter, cover with foil and keep warm in a steam pot or slightly warm oven.

Peel the garlic and put through a garlic press into a ceramic or glass bowl.

COOKING

Heat the oil over medium heat in a small saucepan and add the crushed red pepper. Cook for 5 minutes, then pour through a strainer over the minced garlic. The garlic will sizzle. Add soy sauce, the chicken liquid and Tabasco sauce to the garlic and mix well. Pour the sauce over the chicken and serve. Or serve the sauce separately in little individual dishes as a dip for the chicken.

Steamed Chicken Chilled in Gelatin
4 Servings

This as a good dish to prepare for guests or for a banquet dinner because you can prepare it ahead. Since it is served chilled there is no last-minute work.

4 scallions

1 steamed chicken (recipe on page 76)

1½ cups liquid from steamed chicken, chilled

1 package unflavored gelatin

Parsley

PREPARATION

Bone the chicken and cut into attractive serving pieces. Grease an 8-inch pie plate or 8-inch-round vegetable bowl. Cut the scallions in 1-inch pieces or make Scallion Brushes (see page 138). Arrange the scallions attractively on the plate. Then arrange the chicken pieces over the scallions, with the best-looking side down. (You are working upside down; when you unmold the dish the bottom will become the top.)

COOKING

Remove the solidified fat from the top of the chilled chicken liquid. Heat the liquid and add enough water to makes 1½ cups. Add the gelatin and cook over low heat until it dissolves. Let the liquid cool a little and then pour it over the chicken. Weight the chicken pieces with a small plate, and chill.

Unmold on a flat plate. If the gelatin sticks, dip the bowl briefly in hot water, being careful not to let any water get into the bowl. Garnish with parsley.

Diced Chicken with Mushrooms
4 Servings

This chicken dish is very tasty but not spicy. If you want to vary the flavor, use veal instead of chicken. To make dicing easier, freeze the chicken first and then defrost slightly.

2 boneless chicken breasts,
  partially frozen
2 tablespoons soy sauce
1 tablespoon water
¼ teaspoon white pepper
4 teaspoons cornstarch
¼ cup corn oil

½ cup chicken broth
2 cloves garlic
½ cup water chestnuts
2 cups mushrooms*
½ cup dry-roasted peanuts
  or cashews

PREPARATION

Dice the chicken (⅜-inch cubes) and marinate in a mixture of soy sauce, water, white pepper, 2 teaspoons cornstarch, and 1 teaspoon corn oil for 15 minutes.

Combine the chicken broth and remaining 2 teaspoons of cornstarch in a small bowl. Peel the garlic. Dice the water chestnuts and mushrooms.

COOKING

Put 1½ tablespoons of the corn oil in a wok or pan and set over medium-high heat. When the oil is hot, put in the garlic. When the garlic turns brown, remove it and put in the diced mushrooms and water chestnuts. Cook, stirring and turning, for 1 minute. Remove with a slotted spoon and wipe the wok with paper towels.

Put the rest of the oil in the wok and heat until the oil is almost smoky. Put in the marinated chicken and cook, stirring and turning, until the chicken changes color and cooks through. Stir the cornstarch mixture and add it slowly to the chicken gravy, stirring until the gravy thickens. Return the vegetables to the wok, combine well, and cook 1 minute. Serve topped with the nuts.

NOTE

You can freeze uncooked marinated chicken for later use. Or cook the vegetables and chicken slightly and store separately. Do not combine until you are ready to reheat.

* SUBSTITUTION

Chinese black mushrooms, ½ cup soaked (2 tablespoons dried), can be used instead of the fresh mushrooms (see page 26).

Diced Chicken and Cashews
4 Servings

This is a basic recipe that you can vary simply by using different Chinese flavorings. The red and green peppers make it pretty.

2 boneless chicken breasts, partially frozen	2 tablespoons soy sauce
¼ teaspoon white pepper	1 tablespoon water
1½ teaspoons cornstarch	1 tablespoon dry vermouth
½ cup bamboo shoots	½ cup canned button mushrooms*
½ cup green peppers	1 recipe Mock Hoisin Sauce (recipe page 84)
½ cup red peppers	½ cup dry-roasted cashews
2 garlic cloves	
3 tablespoons corn oil	

PREPARATION
Dice the chicken (⅜-inch cubes) and marinate in a mixture of soy sauce, water, pepper, and cornstarch.

Dice the bamboo shoots and the green and red peppers. Peel the garlic.

COOKING
Put the corn oil in a wok or pan and set over medium-high heat. When the oil is hot, put in the garlic. When the garlic browns, discard it and put in the chicken. Cook, stirring, until the chicken changes color and cooks through. Add the vermouth and cook 30 seconds more. Remove the chicken with a slotted spoon, leaving the oil and liquid in the wok. Add the mushrooms and diced vegetables and cook, turning, until they are heated through. Return the chicken to the wok with the vegetables. Add 2 tablespoons Mock Hoisin Sauce. Combine well, cook 1 minute, and serve, topped with cashews.

* SUBSTITUTION
Chinese black mushrooms (see page 26), soaked and diced, can take the place of canned mushrooms.

NOTE

Uncooked marinated chicken can be frozen, but vegetables will become soggy if frozen. To get a head start on this dish, marinate and refrigerate the chicken a day ahead. The vegetables can be cut and refrigerated a day ahead also, if you store them in plastic bags with paper towels inside to absorb the moisture.

Hoisin sauce (see page 28) has a distinctive taste that will make this dish a little tangy, but not hot. If you prefer, add 2 tablespoons instead of the Mock Hoisin. If you want the dish to be spicy-hot, add 2 tablespoons of Sze-Chuan hot bean sauce (see page 30) instead. Or use 1 tablespoon of each. Each region of China would serve this dish in a different way. Northerners would use the Hoisin sauce. For the eastern taste it would be served with sweet bean paste. Sze-Chuan hot bean sauce would be used in the west. For Chinese southern-style cooking, no sauce is added.

Mock Hoisin Sauce

2 tablespoons peanut butter	⅛ teaspoon garlic powder
4 tablespoons soy sauce	2 teaspoons sesame-seed oil
1 tablespoon honey	20 drops of Red Hot sauce
2 teaspoons white vinegar	⅛ teaspoon white pepper

Combine all ingredients and mix well.

Sliced Chicken with Asparagus
4 Servings

When fresh asparagus is in season this is an outstanding dish. However, when the fresh variety is not available you can make it with frozen asparagus. Do not use canned asparagus.

2 boneless chicken breasts,
partially frozen
½ cup plus 2 tablespoons
chicken broth
¼ teaspoon white pepper
¾ teaspoon salt

3½ teaspoons cornstarch
1½ pounds asparagus
1 large carrot
1 garlic clove
¼ cup corn oil

PROCESSING

Pack the partially frozen chicken breasts upright in the feed tube with the slicing disk in place. Process with pressure to get uniform slices.

ADDITIONAL PREPARATION

Marinate the chicken in a mixture of 2 tablespoons chicken broth, pepper, ½ teaspoon salt, and 2 teaspoons cornstarch for at least 15 minutes.

Combine the remaining ½ cup chicken broth and 1½ cornstarch in a small bowl.

Remove the white ends of the asparagus. Slice the spears diagonally, ¼ inch thick. Scrape the carrot and slice it diagonally as you did the asparagus, but make the carrot slices a little thinner since it is a firmer vegetable and so takes more time to cook. Peel the garlic.

COOKING

Put the corn oil in a wok or pan over medium-high heat. When the oil is hot, put in the garlic clove. When the garlic turns brown remove it and put in the asparagus and carrot slices. Add the remaining ¼ teaspoon salt and cook, stirring and turning, 1 minute. Remove to a dish with a slotted spoon, leaving the oil in the wok. Add the chicken slices and cook quickly, stirring, until they change color and cook through, about 2 minutes. Stir the chicken-broth-and-cornstarch mixture and add it to the chicken, stirring until the sauce thickens. Return the asparagus and carrots to the wok, combine well and serve.

Sliced Chicken with Snow-Pea Pods
4 Servings

Fresh snow-pea pods are the most desirable, but when you cannot get them, the frozen ones aren't bad at all if you handle them right. The ingredients for this dish are the same whether you use fresh or frozen pea pods, but the amount of oil will vary and the cooking technique is different. I will tell you how to make this dish both ways, first with fresh pea pods.

2 boneless chicken breasts partially frozen	**2 cups fresh snow-pea pods (or 1 package frozen pea pods)**
4 ounces water chestnuts	**1 garlic clove**
1 tablespoon soy sauce	**¼ cup corn oil (or 3 tablespoons corn oil if you use frozen pea pods)**
½ cup plus 2 tablespoons chicken broth	
¼ teaspoon white pepper	
2 tablespoons plus 2 teaspoons cornstarch	**¼ teaspoon salt**

PROCESSING
Pack the semifrozen chicken breasts upright in the feed tube with the slicing disk in place. Process with pressure to get uniform slices. Wipe the bowl, replace the slicing disk, pack the feed tube with water chestnuts and process.

ADDITIONAL PREPARATION
Marinate the chicken in a mixture of soy sauce, 2 tablespoons chicken broth, pepper, and 2 teaspoons cornstarch for at least 15 minutes. Remove the strings and stems from the pea pods, wash, and drain, Combine the remaining chicken broth and cornstarch in a small bowl. Peel the garlic.

COOKING
Put the corn oil in a wok or pan over medium-high heat. When the oil is hot, put in the garlic clove. When the garlic turns brown, remove it and put in the pea pods

and water chestnuts. Add salt and cook 30 seconds. Remove with a slotted spoon, leaving the oil in the wok.

Put in the chicken slices and cook quickly, turning and stirring until the chicken changes color and cooks through. Stir the cornstarch mixture and add it slowly, stirring until the gravy thickens. Return the vegetables to the wok with the chicken, combine well and serve.

For Frozen Pea Pods

PREPARATION

Allow the package of pea pods to defrost in the refrigerator until the pods separate from each other but are still frozen. Bring 2 cups of water to a boil. Put the pods in a sieve with a handle and submerge it in the boiling water. Lift out immediately and run it briefly under cold tap water. The pea pods will be crisp.

Prepare other ingredients as described above.

COOKING

Put 3 tablespoons of corn oil in a wok or pan over medium-high heat. When the oil is hot, put in the garlic clove. When the garlic turns brown, remove it and put in the chicken slices. Stir until cooked. Add the cornstarch mixture and stir until the gravy thickens. Add the water chestnuts and blanched pea pods. Combine well, cook 1 minute, and serve.

Sliced Chicken with Broccoli
4 Servings

2 boneless chicken breasts or 1½ cups dark meat, partially frozen

1 cup fresh mushrooms

½ cup plus 1 tablespoon chicken broth

1 tablespoon soy sauce

⅛ teaspoon white pepper

1½ teaspoons cornstarch

1 bunch broccoli

2 garlic cloves

¼ cup corn oil

½ teaspoon salt

1 tablespoon dry white wine

PROCESSING

Pack the chicken breasts upright in the feed tube with the slicing disk in place. Process with pressure to get uniform slices.

Wipe the work bowl, replace the slicing disk, and pack the mushrooms in the feed tube. Process with pressure to get uniform slices.

ADDITIONAL PREPARATION

Marinate the chicken in a mixture of 1 tablespoon chicken broth, soy sauce, white pepper, and I teaspoon cornstarch for 20 minutes.

Mix ¼ cup chicken broth with the remaining ½ teaspoon cornstarch in a small bowl.

Cut the broccoli head into individual flowers. Peel the stringy outer fibers of the stems, and roll-cut. (See sketch on page 32.) Peel the garlic cloves.

COOKING

Put 2 tablespoons of corn oil in a wok or pan over medium-high heat. When the oil is hot, add the salt and then the broccoli. Cook, stirring and turning, for about 2 minutes. If you like softer broccoli, add ¼ cup water and cook for 1 or 2 minutes longer. Add the mushrooms and stir-fry 1 minute. Remove the broccoli and mushrooms to a bowl and wipe the wok with paper towels.

Heat the remaining oil in the wok. Put in the garlic. When the garlic browns, remove it and put in the chicken. Stir-fry until cooked. Add wine and cook 30 seconds. Stir the chicken-broth mixture and add to the chicken. Cook, stirring, until the sauce thickens. Return the vegetables to the wok with the chicken, combine well and serve.

NOTE

You can freeze uncooked marinated chicken for later use. If you are cooking a large quantity, stir-fry the chicken and broccoli ahead of time and store separately. Do not combine until you are ready to reheat.

Sliced Chicken with Green Peppers
 4 Servings

You can make this dish spicy, or eliminate the hot spices. The red sauce, white chicken, and green peppers make it pretty.

2 boneless chicken breasts, partially frozen	1 tablespoon soy sauce
¼ teaspoon white pepper	1 tablespoon chicken broth
1½ teaspoons cornstarch	1 teaspoon chili pepper (optional)
⅓ cup tomato catsup	1 teaspoon Tabasco sauce (optional)
1 tablespoon white vinegar	
1 tablespoon white wine	2 green peppers
1 teaspoon sugar	¼ cup corn oil

PROCESSING
Pack the chicken breasts upright in the feed tube with the slicing disk in place. Process with pressure to get uniform slices.

ADDITIONAL PREPARATION
Marinate the chicken in a mixture of soy sauce, chicken broth, pepper, and cornstarch for 20 minutes.

Combine the catsup, vinegar, wine, sugar, chili pepper, and Tabasco sauce. Wash the green peppers, remove the seeds and white fibers, and cut in pieces measuring 2 inches by ½ inch.

COOKING
Put 1 tablespoon corn oil in a wok or pan over medium-high heat. When the oil is hot, put in the green peppers. Stir-fry 1 minute and remove. Add the remaining oil, and when the oil is hot, put in all the chicken and stir-fry until cooked. Add the sauce mixture, bring it to a boil, and cook for 1 minute so the chicken can absorb the sauce. Return the green peppers to the wok with the chicken, combine well and serve.

NOTE

You can freeze the marinated chicken. Or cook the chicken with the sauce ahead of time and add the green peppers when you reheat just before serving.

Chicken Cooked in Soy
4 Servings

This is another basic recipe from the southern region. It is so versatile you will find yourself making it over and over. Serve it hot or cold, using chicken parts or the whole chicken. Save the sauce that you cook it in; keep it in the refrigerator and use it again, just adding more soy sauce, broth, and water. Each time the sauce will be enriched with additional flavor from the chicken.

1 roasting chicken, 3½ to 4 pounds	¾ cup soy sauce
	1 cup chicken broth
2 scallions	½ cup plus 1 teaspoon water
¼ cup dry white wine or vermouth	½ teaspoon cornstarch

PREPARATION

Wash the chicken thoroughly and pat dry. Cut off the scallion bulbs and place in the cavity of the chicken. Chop the greens to use as a garnish.

COOKING

Put the chicken in a large pot with a cover. Pour in the wine or vermouth and set over medium heat. Bring the wine to a boil, cover, and let the chicken steam for 3 minutes. Remove the chicken. Pour off the liquid and discard.

Put the soy sauce, chicken broth, and water into the same pot and bring to a boil. Put the chicken in the boiling liquid, reduce heat, and simmer 20 minutes, turning the chicken once.

To serve hot, wait for the chicken to cool enough to handle and cut into serving pieces. Remove the bones if you like. Heat up some of the liquid to use as gravy and thicken it slightly by adding ½ teaspoon cornstarch mixed with a teaspoon of cold water. Pour over the chicken, top with chopped scallion greens and serve.

To serve cold, wait for the chicken to cool enough to handle. Chop it into small pieces with bones, the Chinese style. Or remove the bones and cut into small pieces. Arrange on a serving dish and pour over enough of the liquid to moisten the chicken pieces. Top with scallion greens and refrigerate covered with foil, until you are ready to serve.

Cooked chicken can be stored up to 2 or 3 days wrapped in foil and refrigerated. Refrigerate the sauce in a glass jar and remove the fat that solidifies at the top of the sauce when it chills. Reheat the sauce for gravy, or use it again to cook more chicken. Add more soy sauce, chicken broth, and water, in the correct proportions, as needed.

Chicken Cubes with Onions
4 Servings

This is a delicious dish made with dark meat, which is preferred by Oriental people. I suggest that the skin and bones be removed because it is healthier not to eat the skin, and safer not to have chipped bones in the dish. The authentic Chinese way is to chop and cook the chicken pieces with the bones. Save the bones for soup.

4 whole chicken legs, or 8 thighs	2 medium onions
3½ tablespoons soy sauce	2 tablespoons corn oil
2 teaspoons cornstarch	2 tablespoons dry white wine or vermouth
⅓ cup water	½ teaspoon sugar
2 garlic cloves	

PREPARATION
Remove the skin and cut the chicken from the bones in 1-inch cubes. Marinate the chicken pieces for 20

minutes in a mixture of 2 tablespoons soy sauce, cornstarch, and 3 tablespoons water. Mix the rest of the soy
sauce with 3 tablespoons water in a small dish.

Peel the garlic cloves and chop with the steel blade.
Peel the onions, cut crosswise in half, and cut each half in
quarters. Separate the layers of the onions.

COOKING

Put the onions and the rest of the water into a saucepan, cover, bring to a boil, and simmer until the onions
are slightly soft.

Heat the corn oil in the wok over high heat. Put in
the garlic. When the garlic turns a light brown, remove
and add the marinated chicken. Stir-fry until the chicken
changes color. Pour in the wine or vermouth, cover and
cook 30 seconds. Add the onions, the soy-sauce-and-
water mixture, and the sugar. Mix well, cover, and cook 3
more minutes.

NOTE

This dish can be cooked ahead. Reheat quickly
over high heat.

Authentic Version

Replace the onions with 30 dried soaked tiger-lily
buds and ⅓ cup soaked dried tree ears (see page 30).
This is a favorite southern recipe.

Fried Chicken Chinese Style
4 Servings

Since everybody loves fried chicken, this recipe allows half a chicken for each serving. The Chinese call
fried chicken "deep-fry eight pieces" because each
chicken is traditionally cut into eight pieces.

2 scallions	2 tablespoons cornstarch
2 frying chickens	⅛ teaspoon anise powder
1 egg white	2 tablespoons salt
6 tablespoons soy sauce	2 tablespoons white pepper
1 tablespoon dry white wine	4 cups corn oil

PROCESSING

Cut the scallions in 1½-inch pieces and put in the work bowl with the steel blade. Turn the motor on and off quickly 2 or 3 times to chop.

ADDITIONAL PREPARATION

Disjoint the chickens. Save the back bones for soup. If you split the breasts in two, you should get 8 pieces from each chicken. Wash and pat dry. Beat the egg white until just frothy. Add the scallions, soy sauce, wine, and cornstarch, and anise powder, and marinate the chicken pieces in this mixture for 30 minutes or more.

Mix the salt and pepper to use as a dip.

COOKING

Heat the oil to 375 degrees F. Deep-fry chicken until light golden brown. Lift out onto paper towels. Raise the temperature of the oil to 400 degrees F. and deep-fry the chicken again until dark golden brown. Serve with the salt-and-pepper mixture on the side.

NOTE

Since the chicken is fried twice, you can do the first frying ahead of time and the second just before serving. You can also freeze the chicken after you fry it the first time. Defrost and refry just before serving.

Crispy Chicken
4 Servings

This is another way of frying chicken. When you fry it whole, the skin of the chicken is stretched and becomes light and crisp.

1 whole frying chicken	1 tablespoon dry white wine
¼ teaspoon ginger powder	2 scallions
⅛ teaspoon anise powder	4 cups corn oil
5 tablespoons soy sauce	

PREPARATION

Wash the chicken and pat dry. Mix the ginger, anise, soy sauce, and wine. Pour over the chicken, rub in well, and marinate for at least one hour.

Reserve the scallion bulbs for another dish. With the steel blade, chop the greens to use as a garnish.

COOKING

Steam the chicken in its marinade for 20 minutes. Cool on a rack and use paper towels to absorb the excess moisture.

Heat the corn oil in a wok to 375 degrees F. The wok's round bottom makes it ideal for holding the chicken. For this dish, when the oil reaches the proper temperature, place the wok on its ring over the flame for more stability. Deep-fry the chicken until brown and crisp. Lift it out, drain on paper towels, and cut in serving pieces. Garnish with chopped scallion greens.

Shredded Chicken with Bean Sprouts
4 Servings

This is a dish of contrasting textures, tender chicken and crisp bean sprouts. You must use fresh bean sprouts (see page 155), and the results will be more elegant if you take the time to remove their stringy tails. The ham and scallions add color to the dish and make it beautiful as well as delicious.

2 boneless, skinless chicken breasts, partially frozen
¼ pound cooked ham, sliced ⅛ inch thick
1 egg white
1½ teaspoons salt
1½ teaspoons cornstarch
1½ pounds fresh bean sprouts
4 scallions
¼ cup corn oil
2 tablespoons soy sauce
2 tablespoons hot oil

PROCESSING

Slice the partially frozen chicken breasts diagonally across the grain. Make slices ⅛ inch thick. Pack the slices on edge in the feed tube with the slicing disk in place and process with pressure to get uniform shreds. Remove to a dish and wipe the work bowl. Place the ham slices on end in the feed tube and shred in the same way.

ADDITIONAL PREPARATION

Beat the egg white with ¾ teaspoon salt until frothy. Combine with chicken and add the cornstarch. Marinate for about 15 minutes.

Pick over the bean sprouts and remove their stringy tails.

Reserve the scallion bulbs for another dish. Cut the greens into 2-inch pieces. If they are large, split each piece lengthwise.

COOKING

Heat 1 tablespoon corn oil in a wok or pan. Put in all the bean sprouts and quickly toss and turn over high heat for 1 minute. Sprinkle with ¾ teaspoon salt and remove immediately from the wok.

Discard the liquid in the wok, rinse it, wipe dry, and set over medium-high heat. Put in the rest of the oil and when the oil is hot, add the marinated chicken. Stir and turn until it is cooked through. Return the bean sprouts to the wok with the chicken and combine well.

Place on a serving dish and garnish with the shredded ham and the scallions. Serve with small dishes of soy sauce and hot oil (see page 28) on the side. Chinese people would eat this dish without additional seasonings, for the sheer pleasure of the contrast in textures. But so many people enjoy spicy-hot foods, I suggest that you make extra seasonings available.)

Chicken Soong with Pine Nuts
4 Servings

Soong means "minced," so that tells you right away what kind of dish this is. It's delicious, but with all the mincing you have to do, you need either a food processor or lots of patience. Wrapping the chicken in lettuce leaves is half the fun of eating this dish.

½ cup red pepper*
½ cup green pepper*
½ cup water chestnuts
½ cup celery
2 boneless chicken breasts, partially frozen
2 tablespoons chicken broth
2 tablespoons soy sauce
⅛ teaspoon white pepper

2 teaspoons cornstarch
2 cloves garlic
1 small head lettuce
¼ cup corn oil
¾ teaspoon salt
2 tablespoons dry white wine
½ cup pine nuts, roasted

PROCESSING

Cut the red and green peppers into 1½-inch pieces and put them in the work bowl with the steel blade. Mince by turning the motor on and off quickly a few times. Remove the peppers to a dish. Mince the water chestnuts, then the celery, in the same way. Wipe the bowl.

Cut the partially frozen chicken into uniform pieces and mince the same way. Be careful not to overprocess or you will have chicken paste.

* SUBSTITUTION

Hot red peppers and hot green peppers can be substituted if you prefer them.

ADDITIONAL PREPARATION

Marinate the chicken in a mixture of chicken broth, soy sauce, pepper, and cornstarch for at least 20 minutes.

Peel the garlic cloves and put them through a garlic press. Wash the lettuce, separate the leaves, pat dry, and refrigerate.

COOKING

Heat 1½ tablespoon of the corn oil in a pan or wok. When the oil is hot, add the salt, then all of the minced vegetables. Stir-fry for 2 minutes. Remove to a dish and wipe the wok with paper towels.

Put the rest of the oil in the wok over high heat. When the oil is hot, add the marinated chicken and stir-fry for 1 minute. Add the garlic and wine, mix and stir for a few seconds. Return the vegetables to the wok with the chicken, combine well, and cook another minute to heat through. Top with pine nuts and serve on a platter surrounded with the lettuce-leaf cups.

Let each person serve himself, spooning some Chicken Soong into a lettuce cup, wrapping it and eating it like a sandwich.

NOTE

The marinated minced chicken can be frozen until ready to be used. Reheating the whole dish will not spoil it but the taste and texture won't be quite as good.

6
Beef Main Dishes

Beef and Broccoli
4 Servings

I always teach this dish to my students in their first class because it is so fundamental and good, I serve it at home nearly every week.

1 pound lean beef, partially frozen (flank steak, sirloin, or round steak; if you use top or bottom round, treat it with ¼ teaspoon unflavored meat tenderizer)
3 tablespoons soy sauce

5 tablespoons water
⅛ teaspoon white pepper
2½ teaspoons cornstarch
¼ cup chicken broth
1 bunch broccoli
⅓ cup corn oil
½ teasepoon salt

* SUBSTITUTIONS
2 tablespoons oyster sauce (see page 29) can be used instead of the gravy mixture. It will give added flavor to the dish. ½ teaspoon Tabasco sauce can be added to the gravy for a spicy touch.

PROCESSING

Cut partially frozen meat into chunks 2 inches by ¾ inch, to fit the feed tube. Cut so that the meat will be sliced across the grain. With the slicing disk in place, process with pressure to get uniform ⅛-inch slices.

ADDITIONAL PREPARATION

Marinate the beef in a mixture of 2½ tablespoons soy sauce, 2 tablespoons water, pepper, and 2 teaspoons cornstarch for at least half an hour.

Combine the chicken broth with ½ teaspoon cornstarch and ½ tablespoon soy sauce as a gravy mixture.

Wash the broccoli, cut the flowers from the stems, and separate into individual flowerets. Peel the stems, remove the tough fibers, and cut into ¼-inch slices.

COOKING

Heat 2 tablespoons corn oil in a wok. Add broccoli all at once, sprinkle with salt, and turn while cooking. Add 3 tablespoons water. The water will create steam to help make the broccoli tender. Cook to the degree of crispness you prefer, then remove the broccoli to a dish.

Wipe the wok with a paper towel, put in the rest of the oil, and set over high heat. When the oil is hot, put in the beef and stir-fry until it cooks through and turns brown. Stir the chicken-broth mixture and pour it over the meat. Cook, stirring, until the sauce thickens. Return the broccoli to the wok, combine well, and serve.

NOTE

The meat can be sliced and marinated the day before. You can even freeze the marinated meat for future use.

Beef and Snow-Pea Pods
   4 Servings

This is a variation of the previous recipe, Beef and Broccoli. You can use the same cooking method with other vegetables as well.

1 pound lean beef, partially frozen (flank steak, sirloin, top or bottom round; if you use round steak, treat it with ¼ teaspoon unflavored meat tenderizer)	2½ teaspoons cornstarch
	2 tablespoons water
	⅛ teaspoon white pepper
	¼ cup chicken broth
	2 cups snow-pea pods, fresh or frozen*
	⅓ cup corn oil
3 tablespoons soy sauce	½ teaspoon salt

PROCESSING
Cut meat with the grain into chunks 2 inches by ¾ inch, to fit the feed tube. Process with pressure to get uniform ⅛-inch slices, across the grain.

ADDITIONAL PREPARATION
Marinate the beef slices in a mixture of 2 tablespoons soy sauce, 2 teaspoons cornstarch, 2 tablespoons water, and the pepper for at least 20 minutes.

Mix the chicken broth with ½ teaspoon cornstarch and 1 tablespoon soy sauce as a gravy mixture.

If you use fresh pea pods, remove ends and the strings. If you use frozen pea pods, allow to defrost partially.

COOKING
Heat 2 tablespoons corn oil in a wok. Add the pea pods, sprinkle with salt and cook, stirring and turning, for 1 minute. Remove to a dish and wipe the wok with paper towels.

* SUBSTITUTION
Asparagus or celery, sliced diagonally, can be used instead of pea pods.

Heat the rest of the oil over high heat. When the oil is hot, put in the beef and stir-fry until cooked. Pour in the gravy mixture and stir until it thickens. Return the pea pods to the wok, combine well and serve.

NOTE
Marinated meat can be kept in the refrigerator for a day, or frozen and kept longer.

Shredded Beef and Onions
   4 Servings

Since the beef is shredded, it becomes naturally tenderized. This is a wonderful way to use less expensive cuts of meat and still get maximum enjoyment.

1 pound lean beef, partially frozen (flank steak, sirloin, top, or bottom round)	1 tablespoon cornstarch
	⅓ cup corn oil
	¼ cup chicken broth
	2 tablespoons water
3 tablespoons soy sauce	2 onions
1 tablespoon dry white wine	1 green pepper

PROCESSING
Cut beef with the grain into chunks 2 inches by ¾ inch, to fit the feed tube. Process with pressure to slice, across the grain, into uniform ⅛-inch slices. Stack 4 or 5 slices together and place on edge in the feed tube. Process with pressure for uniform ⅛-inch shreds.

ADDITIONAL PREPARATION
Marinate the beef shreds in a mixture of 2 tablespoons soy sauce, wine, 2 teaspoons cornstarch, and 1 tablespoon corn oil for at least 20 minutes.

Mix the chicken broth, water, 1 tablespoon soy sauce, and 1 teaspoon cornstarch as a gravy mixture.

Cut the onions and green pepper lengthwise into strips to match the meat.

COOKING

Heat the remaining corn oil in a wok over high heat. When the oil is hot, add the marinated meat. Stir-fry until the meat turns from red to brown, then remove it to a dish with a slotted spoon.

Put in the onions and green peppers and stir-fry for a minute. Remove to a dish. Pour the gravy mixture into the wok and cook, stirring, until it thickens. Return the meat and vegetables to the wok, combine well and serve immediately over rice or noodles.

NOTE
This dish freezes well.

Beef and Tomatoes
4 Servings

The ingredients are basic, yet this is a delicious dish.

1 pound lean beef, partially frozen (flank steak, sirloin, top or bottom round; if you use round steak, treat it with ¼ teaspoon unflavored meat tenderizer)	¼ cup water
	2½ teaspoons cornstarch
	¼ teaspoon white pepper
	⅓ cup corn oil
	2 tablespoons chicken broth
	2 medium onions
3 tablespoons soy sauce	4 small tomatoes or 2 or 3 large ones

PROCESSING

Cut the meat with the grain into chunks 2 inches by ¾ inch, to fit the feed tube. Process with pressure to get uniform ⅛-inch slices, across the grain.

ADDITIONAL PREPARATION

Marinate the beef slices in a mixture of 2 tablespoons soy sauce, 2 tablespoons water, 2 teaspoons cornstarch, pepper, and 1 tablespoon corn oil for at least 20 minutes.

Combine 1 tablespoon soy sauce, 2 tablespoons water, ½ teaspoon cornstarch, and the chicken broth as a gravy mixture.

Peel and quarter the onions and separate the layers. Cut the tomatoes into quarters.

COOKING

Heat 2 tablespoons of corn oil over medium-high heat. When the oil is hot, add the onions and tomatoes. Cook, stirring, 1 minute and remove to a dish. Rinse the wok and wipe it dry.

Heat the remaining oil in the wok over high heat. When the oil is hot, put in the marinated beef slices and quickly stir-fry the meat until it browns. Pour in the gravy mixture and stir until it thickens. Add the tomatoes and onions, combine well and serve.

Beef Western Style
4 Servings

This dish—actually Chinese-style steak—is very easy and quick to make. The steaks can also be served on toast as open-face sandwiches.

2½ pounds club steak, cut ¼ inch thick	⅛ teaspoon white pepper
¼ cup water	1 teaspoon cornstarch
1 teaspoon dry white wine	½ head lettuce
1 tablespoon soy sauce	2 tomatoes
	1 tablespoon corn oil

PREPARATION

Trim the fat from the steaks and marinate in a mixture of water, wine, soy sauce, pepper, and cornstarch for at least 20 minutes.

Shred the lettuce and use it to line a serving platter. Cut the tomatoes into wedges and arrange them around the edge of the platter.

COOKING

Heat the corn oil in a large skillet over a high flame. When the oil is hot, brown the steaks on both sides until they reach the doneness you like. Then pour in the marinade and stir until the sauce is cooked. Arrange the steaks on the shredded lettuce, pour the sauce over, and serve.

Beef and Scallions
4 Servings

This is a delicious dish that uses simple ingredients. The authentic method in the western Chinese cuisine is to deep-fry and then combine everything. I prefer to stir-fry, but I have included both methods.

1 pound lean beef, partially frozen (flank steak, sirloin, top or bottom round; if you use round steak, treat it with ¼ teaspoon unflavored meat tenderizer)*	2½ tablespoons soy sauce
	1 tablespoon cornstarch
	¼ teaspoon white pepper*
	¼ cup chicken broth
	½ teaspoon Gravy Master*
	2 bunches scallions
1 egg white	⅓ cup corn oil

PROCESSING

Cut the meat with the grain into chunks 2½ inches long, 2 inches wide, and ¾ inch thick, to fit the feed tube. Process with pressure to get uniform ⅛-inch slices, across the grain.

ADDITIONAL PREPARATION

Beat the egg white slightly. Mix with the beef slices

* SUBSTITUTIONS

Lamb can be used instead of beef. Chili pepper can replace the white pepper for a more spicy flavor. Dark soy can take the place of Gravy Master in the gravy mixture.

and add 2 tablespoons soy sauce, 2 teaspoons cornstarch, and the pepper. Marinate in this mixture for 20 minutes.

Mix the chicken broth with ½ teaspoon soy sauce, 1 teaspoon cornstarch, and the Gravy Master, as a gravy mixture.

Cut the scallions into 2-inch-long pieces.

COOKING

Put the corn oil in a wok over medium-high heat. When the oil is hot, put in all the scallions. Stir and turn for half a minute, then remove with a slotted spoon, leaving the oil in the wok.

Add the beef slices, turn the heat up high, and quickly stir-fry until the meat is just cooked. Add the chicken-broth mixture and keep on stirring until the sauce thickens. Add the scallions, mix well, and serve.

NOTE

The marinated meat can be refrigerated for a day or two, or frozen and kept longer.

Authentic Version

Heat 3 cups of oil to 300 degrees F. Put in the marinated meat and stir with chopsticks to separate the pieces. When the meat turns light brown, remove it with a slotted spoon. Stir-fry the scallions and add the meat, then the gravy mixture. Bring to a boil, allow to thicken slightly, and serve.

Curried Beef
4 Servings

This dish is really a stew, and the good part is that you can cook it ahead of time, then just reheat. I always serve it with plain rice.

2 pounds short ribs or 1½ pounds boneless stewing beef	1 cup chicken broth
	1 cup water
	3 onions
1 tablespoon soy sauce	3 tomatoes
1 tablespoon dry white wine	4 tablespoons curry powder*
¼ teaspoon white pepper	3 tablespoons corn oil
3 tablespoons cornstarch	

PREPARATION

Cut the meat into ¾-inch pieces. Marinate in a mixture of soy sauce, wine, pepper, and 1 tablespoon cornstarch for at least 20 minutes.

Combine the chicken broth with ¾ cup water. Mix 2 tablespoons cornstarch and ¼ cup water.

Cut the onions in half. Cut the tomatoes in quarters.

COOKING

Heat the oil in a deep saucepan or Dutch oven over medium-high heat. When the oil is hot, put in the beef and onions. Stir and cook until the meat is brown. Add the curry powder and mix well. Add the chicken-broth mixture and bring it to a boil. Simmer for about 1 hour, until the beef is tender

Thicken the gravy with the cornstarch-and-water-mixture. Add the tomatoes and cook for 10 minutes more. Serve with rice.

NOTE

This dish can be cooked ahead and frozen.

* SUBSTITUTION

The same amount of Sun-brand curry paste will be a delicious substitute for the curry.

Barbecued Beef
4 Servings

This is barbecued beef with a distinctive flavor. It cooks quickly and is perfect to serve outdoors. You can multiply the amounts for a crowd. Be sure to allow time for overnight marinating so you get maximum flavor.

3 pounds flank steak or fillet	2 tablespoons soy sauce
¼ cup water	1 teaspoon sugar
2 cloves garlic, minced	1 tablespoon cornstarch
¼ teaspoon white pepper	Corn oil for deep frying
	½ cup flour

PREPARATION
Slice meat 2 inches square, 1 inch thick, across the grain. Combine the water, garlic, pepper, soy sauce, sugar, and cornstarch, and pour it over the meat. Poke the meat all over with a fork to allow the marinade to penetrate. Refrigerate the meat in the marinade overnight.

COOKING
Heat the oil to 375 degrees F. Drain the meat and coat lightly with flour. Deep-fry the meat in oil for half a minute. It will be only partially cooked, but the flavor will be sealed in.

To serve, barbecue over a grill or broil about 3 minutes on each side, until crisp and brown.

Steak Cantonese
4 Servings

"Steak Kew" on the menu in a Chinese restaurant means steak in cubes. The cubes of meat are well seasoned, juicy, and tender, served on a bed of green vegetables. Your steak will be just as flavorful with this recipe, especially if you marinate it overnight to let the seasonings penetrate.

2 pounds, beef fillet
2 tablespoons soy sauce
3 tablespoons water
1 teaspoon dry white wine
⅛ teaspoon white pepper
⅛ teaspoon garlic powder
Dash of powdered ginger

1 tablespoon fresh parsley, chopped*
1 tablespoon cornstarch
1 small head lettuce*
4 tablespoons corn oil
½ teaspoon salt

PREPARATION

Trim any fat from the meat. Cut the meat into 1-inch cubes and pour over them a mixture of soy sauce, water, wine, pepper, garlic powder, ginger, parsley, and cornstarch. Marinate overnight in the refrigerator.

Wash the lettuce and separate the leaves. Pat dry.

COOKING

Heat 1 tablespoon of the corn oil in a wok. When the oil is hot, put in the lettuce leaves and sprinkle with salt. Cook, turning the leaves over, until the lettuce is limp, about 2 or 3 minutes. Remove to a serving platter with a slotted spoon, leaving the liquid in the pan. Discard liquid.

Clean the wok, put in the rest of the oil, and set over high heat. Drain the meat. When the oil is hot, put the meat in and keep turning to brown it on all sides. Cook 3 to 5 minutes depending on the degree of doneness you prefer. Arrange the meat cubes on the lettuce leaves and serve.

Shredded Beef and Bean Sprouts
4 Servings

Use fresh bean sprouts with their little tails removed, and this dish becomes very elegant. Canned bean sprouts will not be as appealing. Home-grown bean

* SUBSTITUTIONS

Chinese parsley (coriander) can take the place of regular parsley. Broccoli or asparagus can be used instead of lettuce.

sprouts (see page 155) are pure white and about 3 or 4 inches long. They are out of this world!

1 **pound lean beef (sirloin or round steak), partially frozen**	¼ **teaspoon sugar**
	1 **tablespoon water**
	2 **teaspoons cornstarch**
1 **large carrot, scraped and cut in pieces 2 inches long**	3 **cups fresh bean sprouts**
	2 **scallions**
3 **tablespoons soy sauce**	4 **tablespoons corn oil**
1 **tablespoon dry white wine**	¼ **teaspoon salt**

PROCESSING

Slice the meat ⅛-inch thick, across the grain. Stack 4 or 5 slices and place them on edge in the feed tube, with the slicing disk in place. Process with pressure for uniform shreds. Repeat with the rest of the meat.

Wipe the bowl, insert the shredding disk, and shred the carrot by laying one piece on top of another sidewise.

ADDITIONAL PREPARATION

Marinate the beef shreds in a mixture of soy sauce, wine, sugar, water, and cornstarch.

Pick over the bean sprouts and remove the stringy tails. Wash and drain on paper towels. Cut scallions in 2-inch pieces.

COOKING

Put 1 tablespoon corn oil in a wok and set it over high heat. When the oil is hot, add salt and the bean sprouts. Stir and turn quickly for half a minute and remove to a dish. Discard the liquid in the wok and wipe it dry.

Heat 3 tablespoons corn oil in the wok. Add the marinated meat and cook, stirring and turning, for 1 minute. Add the carrots and scallions and cook another minute. Add the bean sprouts, combine well, and serve immediately. Do not overcook or the bean sprouts will lose their crispness.

NOTE

You can freeze the marinated beef, then thaw and stir-fry. Do not freeze the bean sprouts.

Beef Soong
4 Servings

A long time ago, a famous chef was given a pair of squab to make a dish for his master's banquet. Usually there are ten people at a table for banquet dinners. Squab are considered quite a delicacy, but the chef was concerned about how to serve ten people with just two small birds. He solved the problem by dicing a lot of vegetables, dicing the breast meat of the squab, and stir-frying them together. He called the dish Squab Soong, and it was a great success. From this famous chef we got the inspiration for Pork Soong, Chicken Soong, and Beef Soong, all clever ways to stretch a little meat a long way. I am including Beef Soong here because ground beef is so readily available. With little effort or expense you will have a delicious meal.

2 medium onions	1 pound ground beef*
½ cup mushrooms, canned or fresh*	6 tablespoons soy sauce
	4 tablespoons water
½ cup water chestnuts	¼ teaspoon white pepper
½ cup bamboo shoots	½ teaspoon sugar
2 tablespoons cornstarch	⅓ cup corn oil
¼ cup chicken broth	½ cup canned or cooked fresh peas
1 small head lettuce	

* SUBSTITUTIONS

Chinese black mushrooms (see page 26), soaked and diced, can substitute for the fresh or canned mushrooms. You can use ground pork, chicken, or veal with this recipe. And 2 tablespoons oyster sauce can be used instead of the gravy mixture. (See page 29.)

PROCESSING

Cut the onions in 1-inch chunks and place in the work bowl with the steel blade. Turn the motor on and off quickly once or twice to chop. Remove the onions and repeat with the mushrooms, water chestnuts, and bamboo shoots in succession.

ADDITIONAL PREPARATION

Marinate the ground beef for 20 minutes in a mixture of 4 tablespoons soy sauce, water, pepper, sugar, and 1 tablespoon cornstarch.

Combine the chicken broth with the remaining soy sauce and cornstarch to use as a gravy mixture.

Wash the lettuce, separate the leaves and pat dry. Arrange them around the rim of a large platter.

COOKING

Heat 2 tablespoons corn oil in a wok. Sauté the onions until they are translucent. Add the mushrooms, water chestnuts, and bamboo shoots and cook, stirring until they are heated through, about 1 minute. Remove to a dish.

Wipe the wok clean, add the remaining corn oil, and set it over high heat. When the oil is hot, add the marinated beef. Stir-fry until the meat turns brown. Add the gravy mixture and cook, stirring, until the sauce thickens. Add the cooked peas and all the vegetables. Combine well and arrange in the center of the platter.

To eat, spoon some of the Beef Soong into the center of a lettuce leaf, wrap and eat with the fingers.

NOTE

This dish can be frozen and reheated.

7
Pork Main Dishes

Sweet-and-Sour Pork
4 Servings

This is an easy, yet truly delectable and appealing dish. Deep-frying the pork twice makes it doubly crisp and crunchy. The sauce, which is different from any other sweet-and-sour dish, has been tested many, many times, to perfection. For those who do not care for deep-frying, stir-frying the pork is one alternative. The other is to deep-fry the pork only once and then reheat by broiling.

1 pound (2 cups) lean pork tenderloin*	1 egg
	⅛ teaspoon white pepper
1 tablespoon soy sauce	1½ cups cornstarch
4 tablespoons water	2 green peppers
2 medium tomatoes	⅓ cup white vinegar
1 can (8 ounces) pineapple chunks	¼ cup sugar
	2 teaspoons salt
½ cup tomato catsup	3 cups corn oil

* SUBSTITUTION
Chicken can take the place of pork with equally good results.

PREPARATION

Cut the pork into 1-inch cubes. (This will be easier if the meat is partially frozen.) Combine the soy sauce, 1 tablespoon water, beaten egg, pepper, and 1 tablespoon cornstarch. Pour this over the meat, turn to coat, and marinate at room temperature at least 20 minutes.

Cut green peppers and tomatoes in chunks to match the size of the pork cubes. Drain the pineapple and mix the juice with the catsup, vinegar, sugar, and salt. Mix 1½ tablespoons cornstarch with the remaining 3 tablespoons water.

COOKING

Reserve 3 tablespoons of the oil for stir-frying. Heat the rest to 375 degrees F. While the oil is heating, drain the marinated pork. Put the remaining cornstarch in a paper bag, drop in the pork cubes, and shake to coat thoroughly. Deep-fry the pork cubes in oil until golden brown, then drain on paper towels. (The dish can be made ahead up to this point.)

When ready to serve, deep-fry the pork a second time, to a deep golden brown. Put the reserved corn oil in a wok or pan over medium-high heat. Stir-fry the peppers and tomatoes for 1 minute, remove, and drain. Pour in the sauce mixture and bring it to a boil. Stir in the cornstarch mixture gradually to thicken the sauce. Add pineapples, tomatoes, and green peppers, and heat through. Add the crisp pork cubes, mix well, and serve.

Chinese Spareribs
4 Servings

There are two secrets to making delicious spareribs: allow ample marinating time (at least 24 hours) and use a low oven. Incidentally, if you have eaten spareribs in a Chinese restaurant and wondered what gives them their red color—it's red food coloring. Most restaurants make their spareribs as I describe them here, sometimes adding a little Hoisin sauce (see page 28) to the marinade.

2 garlic cloves	¼ teaspoon white pepper
2 tablespoons honey	3 tablespoons soy sauce
2 tablespoons water	1 sheet spareribs
1 tablespoon white vinegar	

You will also need:
A plastic bag large enough to hold the sheet of spareribs. (If you cannot find one, split the sheet in half and use 2 plastic bags.)

PREPARATION

Chop the garlic coarsely, using the steel blade. Reserve 1 tablespoon each of the honey and water, mix, and set aside to use later for basting.

Mix the garlic with the remaining ingredients. Coat the spareribs with this marinade and put them in the plastic bag. Tie it securely and let stand in the refrigerator at least 24 hours. Turn the bag once or twice so the ribs can soak up the marinade evenly.

COOKING

Heat the oven to 250 degrees F. Put spareribs directly on the oven rack, with a pan of water below to catch any drippings. Roast the spareribs for half an hour. Remove and brush with the honey-and-water mixture. Put the spareribs under the broiler and broil the underside first, then the meaty side, until both sides are crisp and brown.

To serve, separate into individual ribs. The sauce can be any of your favorites. Traditional sauces are chutney, plum sauce, or Hoisin sauce.

NOTE

To prepare ahead, roast the spareribs, brush with the honey and water mixture and freeze. Thaw and broil just before serving.

Roast Pork
4 Servings

Every Chinese delicatessen has its own secret recipe for this very popular staple. It is a good idea to try different delicatessens until one finds the roast pork one prefers. The method of preparation is very similar to that for spare ribs. This recipe will give you results that are very similar to roast pork you might get in a Chinese market.

2 pounds pork or pork tenderloin
2 tablespoons honey
2 tablespoons water
2 tablespoons chicken broth
3 tablespoons soy sauce
2 tablespoons dry white wine

2 garlic cloves, crushed
1 teaspoon white pepper
1 teaspoon white vinegar
2 drops Tabasco sauce
1 tablespoon corn oil

PREPARATION
Cut the meat in half lengthwise. Reserve 1 tablespoon each of the honey and water. Mix all the remaining ingredients except the corn oil, pour over the pork, and poke the meat all over with a fork so the marinade can penetrate deeply. Refrigerate overnight.

COOKING
Heat the oven to 275 degrees F. Roast the pork for about 1 hour or until a meat thermometer inserted in the center of the meat registers well done. Brush with corn oil a few times while roasting. When the meat is done, brush it with the honey-and-water mixture. Slice the pork and serve it hot or cold with any kind of prepared sauce on the side. Plum sauce or mustard would be good choices.

NOTE
Roast pork is often called for as an ingredient in recipes, so it is convenient to store some in the freezer.

Authentic Version

Add 1 tablespoon Hoisin sauce (see page 28) to the marinade.

Mo Shu Pork
4 Servings

Mo Shu Pork is becoming almost as popular in Chinese restaurants as chow mein and egg rolls. But, like chow mein, the Mo Shu Pork served in this country is different from the traditional Chinese version, which is primarily an egg dish flavored with pork and vegetables. The pieces of scrambled egg resemble the Mo Shu flower, which is yellow, and that is how the dish got its name. In China, tiger-lily buds and tree ears are used as vegetables. This version has been adapted for use anywhere in the country, without hard-to-find ingredients.

½ pound lean pork,
   partially frozen*
1 small head cabbage
   (about 1 pound)
½ cup fresh mushrooms*
½ cup bamboo shoots*
3 tablespoons soy sauce

1 teaspoon cornstarch
4 scallions
3 eggs
1 tablespoon chicken broth
⅓ cup corn oil
½ teaspoon salt

PROCESSING
Cut chunks of meat to fit the feed tube. With the slicing disk in place, process with pressure, to slice across the grain. Stack 4 or 5 slices together, stand them on edge

* SUBSTITUTIONS
Veal or chicken can be used in place of the pork. Instead of the bamboo shoots and mushrooms, use 30 dried tiger-lily buds and 2 tablespoons dried tree ears (see page 30). Both should be soaked for at least an hour. Cut the tiger-lily buds in 2-inch pieces.

in the feed tube, and process with pressure to get uniform shreds.

Cut chunks of cabbage to fit the feed tube and process with the slicing disk. Pack the feed tube with mushrooms, and slice. Switch to the shredding disk and shred the bamboo shoots.

ADDITIONAL PREPARATION

Marinate the pork for 20 minutes in 2 tablespoons of the soy sauce mixed with the cornstarch.

Cut the scallions into 2-inch lengths, keeping the white and green parts separate. Beat the eggs with the chicken broth.

COOKING

Heat 3 tablespoons corn oil in the wok. Put in the scallion whites, cabbage, bamboo shoots, mushrooms and salt, and stir-fry for 2 minutes. Remove the vegetables to a dish and wipe the wok with a paper towel.

Put in 2 tablespoons corn oil, and when the oil is hot, add the pork and stir-fry for 3 minutes. Return the vegetables to the wok with the pork and mix well. Add 1 tablespoon soy sauce or more if you like.

Set a frying pan over medium heat with 1 tablespoon oil in it. When the oil is hot, pour in the egg mixture and scramble until the egg is set. Add to the meat and vegetables. Mix well, breaking up the egg into small pieces as you do so. Serve topped with the scallion greens.

NOTE

This dish is usually served with Mandarin Pancakes (recipe on page 140). Each person puts a pancake on his plate, fills it with Mo Shu Pork, rolls it up, and eats it like a sandwich.

Vegetables and meat can be prepared ahead. Scramble the egg at the last minute, combine, and serve.

Deep-Fried Spareribs
4 Servings

The crispness of spareribs cooked in this way makes them quite different from roast spareribs. My family loves them, and even though I don't like to do too much deep-frying, the memory of the taste lingers and I can't help repeating the dish.

3 pounds spareribs
(have the butcher cut
through them to make
1½-inch ribs)
3½ tablespoons soy sauce
¼ teaspoon white pepper
1 tablespoon dry white wine

2½ teaspoons cornstarch
1 tablespoon water
2 teaspoons sugar
1 tablespoon white vinegar
3 scallions
2 cups corn oil

PREPARATION

Separate the spareribs into individual pieces. Marinate in a mixture of 1½ tablespoons soy sauce, pepper, wine, and ½ teaspoon cornstarch.

Mix the remaining 2 tablespoons soy sauce, water, sugar, and vinegar, and set aside. Chop the scallions, keeping the white and green parts separate.

COOKING

Reserve 1½ tablespoons corn oil. Heat the rest of the oil to 375 degrees F. Drain the spareribs and coat with the remaining cornstarch. Deep-fry the ribs to a dark golden brown. Drain on paper towels.

Heat the reserved oil in a wok or pan. Put in the scallion whites, and when they are brown, add the soy-sauce mixture. Bring to a boil and add the fried spareribs. Toss to coat the sauce all over the ribs. Sprinkle with the scallion greens and serve. An alternate way is to serve the sauce as a dip with the Deep-Fried Spareribs.

NOTE

Marinated spareribs can be frozen and deep-fried just before serving.

Shredded Pork and Bamboo Shoots
4 Servings

When pork is shredded, you can cook it quickly and still be sure that it is cooked through. If you like hot foods, be sure to include the chili powder and Tabasco sauce.

1 pound lean pork, partially frozen
1½ cups bamboo shoots
3 tablespoons soy sauce
2 tablespoons cornstarch
⅛ teaspoon white pepper

2 scallions
3 tablespoons corn oil
⅛ teaspoon chili powder (optional)
1 tablespoon Tabasco sauce (optional)

PROCESSING
Cut the pork into chunks to fit the feed tube. With the slicing tube in place, process with pressure to make uniform slices, across the grain. Stack several slices and place on edge in the feed tube. Process with pressure for uniform shreds.

Change to the shredding disk, pack the feed tube with bamboo shoots, and process.

ADDITIONAL PREPARATION
Mix the pork with the soy sauce, cornstarch, and pepper, and marinate 20 minutes.

Chop the scallion bulbs. Cut the green parts in 2-inch lengths.

COOKING
Heat corn oil in the wok over high heat. Add the scallion whites and, when they are lightly brown, add the marinated pork. Stir and turn until the pork changes color and is well cooked. Add the chili powder and Tabasco and remove to a serving dish.

Put the bamboo shoots in the wok and heat through. Return the pork to the wok with the bamboo shoots. Toss to combine. Serve topped with scallion greens.

NOTE

Since there are no fresh vegetables in this dish to wilt, you can freeze it and reheat it, after thawing, in the wok.

Shredded Pork and Green Beans
4 Servings

This basic recipe combines shredded pork with a vegetable of your choice. The pork is shredded so it can be cooked quickly and still be well done. The vegetable, whether fresh or frozen, should be cut to match the pork shreds.

1 pound lean pork, partially frozen	3½ teaspoons cornstarch
	¼ cup chicken broth
2 cups French-style green beans, fresh or frozen*	1 tablespoon water
	4 tablespoons corn oil
3 tablespoons soy sauce	¼ teaspoon salt

PROCESSING

Cut the pork into chunks to fit the feed tube. With the slicing disk in place, process with pressure to make uniform slices across the grain. Stack several slices and place on edge in the feed tube. Process with pressure for uniform shreds.

ADDITIONAL PREPARATION

If you use frozen green beans, thaw just until they can be separated. If you use fresh green beans, wash them, cut off the stems, and slice thinly on the diagonal.

Marinate the pork in a mixture of 2 tablespoons soy sauce and 2 teaspoons cornstarch for 20 minutes.

* SUBSTITUTION

Shredded celery or fresh bean sprouts make good alternates to green beans. Do not combine both vegetables for this dish.

Combine the chicken broth, water, and remaining soy sauce and cornstarch.

COOKING
Heat 1 tablespoon corn oil over high heat in the wok. Put in the green beans and salt. Cook, stirring, until the beans reach the degree of tenderness you prefer. If you like your vegetables soft, add a spoonful or two of water; the steam will help cook the vegetable. Remove the beans to a dish and wipe out the wok with a paper towel.

Heat the remaining oil, put in the pork and stir-fry until it changes color and is cooked through. Remove to a dish.

Bring the chicken-broth mixture to a boil in the wok. Return the beans and pork to the wok and combine with the sauce.

NOTE
Marinated or cooked pork can be frozen. To serve, cook the vegetable and sauce and combine with the stir-fried or reheated pork.

Egg Crescents
4 Servings

This dish is traditionally served on the Chinese New Year. The thin egg crepes, stuffed with pork and folded in half, reminded the early Chinese of the money purses they carried, so the crescents are a symbol of good fortune and a full purse in the year to come. The taste is delicate and delicious. Egg Crescents are still another good way to serve a satisfying main dish with a small amount of meat.

½ cup fresh mushrooms*   1¼ cups chicken broth
½ cup bamboo shoots   ⅛ teaspoon white pepper
2 scallions   3 tablespoons soy sauce
5 large eggs   1 teaspoon cornstarch
½ pound (1 cup) ground   1 pound fresh spinach*
  pork   1 tablespoon corn oil

PROCESSING
Put the mushrooms in the work bowl with the steel blade and turn the motor on and off once or twice to chop. Remove and repeat with the bamboo shoots and then the scallions.

ADDITIONAL PREPARATION
Beat the eggs. Mix the ground pork with the mushrooms, bamboo shoots, and scallions, ¼ cup of the chicken broth, pepper, and 2 tablespoons soy sauce.

Mix the rest of the chicken broth with the remaining tablespoon of soy sauce and the cornstarch. Wash and drain the spinach.

COOKING
Use either a wok or a 4-inch frying pan for this step. Set it over low heat and dip a brush in oil to coat the pan or the bottom of the wok. Pour in a tablespoon of the beaten egg and rotate the pan to make a small round crepe. Before the egg sets completely, put a tablespoon of the meat filling in the center of the crepe. Fold it in half and press the edges together. Turn over to brown the other side lightly. Lift the filled crepe onto a dish and repeat until all of the egg batter and filling are used up. You should have about 12 Egg Crescents. At this stage the filling is only partially cooked.

Stir the chicken-broth mixture and pour it into the

* SUBSTITUTIONS
Soak 1 tablespoon Chinese black mushrooms (see page 26) for an hour, remove the stems, and add instead of the fresh mushrooms. Chinese, Napa, or celery cabbage can be used instead of the spinach.

wok or a large saucepan. Bring to a boil, stirring. When the sauce has thickened, gently place the crescents in the pan. Cover and simmer for 5 minutes. Add the spinach, cover, and cook 2 minutes longer. Remove from the heat.

Arrange the spinach on a large dish and the Egg Crescents on top. Cover with the sauce and serve.

NOTE
The partially cooked Egg Crescents can be frozen, or the whole dish can be made ahead of time and reheated.

8
Seafood Main Dishes

Steamed Whole Fish
2 Servings

Whole fish with the head on is full of symbolism in China. Whole stands for wholesomeness. The word for fish in Chinese sounds like the word for overflowing. Thus a whole fish represents a marvelous abundance, like "my cup runneth over" in the Bible. For this reason a whole fish is usually served as the last course of a banquet dinner.

It is really a shame to fillet a nice fresh fish, especially a small one. Chinese people prefer to serve fish with the bones because it is sweeter.

The average family may not have a pot large enough to hold more than one fish for steaming. A 2-pound fish would be the maximum, I think, for home steamers. So you should either steam a fish as the main course for two people or serve fish with another main course for four to six people.

Bass, trout, pike, whiting, fluke, croaker, butterfish,

and whitefish are all good choices for this recipe. There are probably many more that would also be good. Just don't choose an oily fish or one with very firm meat.

2 scallions	½ cup chicken broth
2 tablespoons fresh mushrooms*	1 tablespoon soy sauce
	1 tablespoon corn oil
1 whole fish, 1½ to 2 pounds	Dash of ginger powder*

PROCESSING
Put the scallions, cut in 1½-inch lengths, into the work bowl with the steel blade and chop by turning the motor on and off once or twice. Switch to the slicing disk, pack the mushrooms into the feed tube, and process with pressure.

PREPARATION
Wash and clean the fish. To save work, choose a heat-proof dish in which you can both steam and serve the fish. Cut the fish in half if it is too large to fit in the dish.

Combine the chicken broth, soy sauce, oil, and ginger powder.

COOKING
Bring about 6 cups of water to a boil. Dip the fish in and lift it out immediately. This rinses it to remove the fishy odor.

Put the fish in your heat-proof dish, top with scallions and mushrooms, and pour the chicken broth mixture around the fish. Put the dish on a rack in your largest pot, with 1½ inches of water in the bottom. Cover, bring the water to a boil, and steam over high heat 15 to 20

* SUBSTITUTIONS
Chinese black mushrooms and fresh ginger slices can be used instead of the fresh mushrooms and ginger powder. (See pages 26–27.)

minutes, depending on the size of the fish. Serve piping hot.

NOTE
You can blanch the fish, arrange it on the heat-proof dish, and get it ready for steaming, then refrigerate it for a few hours. Do the steaming just before serving.

Fillet of Fish Cantonese
4 Servings

This is a recipe that I developed, which is always a hit with my students. It is as easy as ABC.

4 scallions*	2 tablespoons corn oil
⅓ cup soy sauce	1 teaspoon salt
⅓ cup chicken broth	1½ pounds of fish fillets
½ teaspoon sugar	(haddock, flounder, or
⅓ cup plus 1 tablespoon	sole, preferably fresh),
water	cut in 4-inch pieces
1 teaspoon cornstarch	

PREPARATION
Chop the scallions, keeping the white and green parts separate. Mix the soy sauce, chicken broth, sugar, and ⅓ cup water. Mix the cornstarch with 1 tablespoon water.

COOKING
Heat the corn oil in a small saucepan. Add the scallion whites and cook until they are light brown. Add the soy-sauce mixture and bring it to a boil. Thicken with the cornstarch mixture and keep the sauce warm.

Bring 4 cups of water to a boil, add the salt, and

* SUBSTITUTION
A tablespoon of fresh ginger (see page 27), minced, will give the sauce added flavor.

regulate the heat to keep the water simmering. Drop the pieces of fish into the water. When the fish becomes flaky, lift out the pieces with a slotted spoon and arrange them on a serving dish. Pour the sauce over and serve, garnished with the scallion greens.

NOTE
You can make the sauce ahead of time and reheat it before serving. The poaching of the fish takes no time at all.

Sweet-and-Sour Fish
4 Servings

1½ pounds fish fillets
(haddock, sole, flounder,
yellow pike, or whiting,
preferably fresh) cut in
3-inch pieces*
2 tablespoons dry white
wine
¼ teaspoon white pepper
2 tablespoons plus 2
teaspoons cornstarch

1 cup flour
1¼ cups water
1½ teaspoons baking
powder
½ cup sugar
½ cup white vinegar
½ cup catsup
2 teaspoons salt
1 green pepper, diced
1 carrot, diced

PREPARATION
Marinate the fish in a mixture of wine, pepper, and 2 teaspoons cornstarch for 20 minutes.

Make a batter by combining 1 cup flour, 1 cup water, and 1½ teaspoons baking powder and mixing until smooth.

Mix the sugar, vinegar, catsup, and salt in a dish.

Mix 2 tablespoons cornstarch and ¼ cup water in another dish.

* SUBSTITUTION
Scallops and shrimp are also delicious cooked this way.

COOKING

Heat the corn oil to 375 degrees F. Dip the pieces of fish into the batter and deep-fry until they are golden brown. Keep warm in a low oven.

Bring the catsup sauce to a boil. Stir the cornstarch mixture and gradually add it to the sauce to thicken it. Add the green peppers and carrot and cook for 1 minute. Pour over the fish and serve.

Red-Cooked Fish
4 Servings

This is a dish from the eastern region. Red-cooking means cooking in soy sauce, and it makes a very flavorful dish. The result will be more tasty if you cook the fish with the bones.

4 garlic cloves	⅓ cup chicken broth
4 scallions	3 tablespoons corn oil
⅓ cup soy sauce	¼ cup dry white wine
4 pieces fresh fish, about ⅓ pound each	1 tablespoon sugar (less if you prefer)
⅓ cup water	

PREPARATION

Peel the garlic. Chop the scallions, keeping the white and green parts separate.

Pour 2 tablespoons of soy sauce over the fish and let it stand for at least an hour.

Mix the rest of the soy sauce with water and chicken broth.

COOKING

Heat the corn oil in a wok or Teflon pan. (The fish skin will stay intact if you use Teflon.) Put in the garlic and scallion whites. When the garlic is brown, add the pieces of fish. Pan-fry both sides of each piece to a golden brown. Add the wine and cook for 2 or 3 minutes. Add the soy-sauce mixture, lower the heat, cover, and cook for 15 minutes. Turn the fish over a few times as it cooks so that all sides will get in contact with the liquid, even though some of the sauce will evaporate. Add sugar and cook 5 more minutes. Serve hot.

NOTE
Reheating will not change the flavor and texture, so you can prepare this dish even a day ahead.

Stir-Fried Shrimp with Water Chestnuts
4 Servings

2 garlic cloves	1 can (8 ounces) water
2 scallions	chestnuts
1½ pounds fresh shrimp,	3 tablespoons corn oil
cleaned and deveined*	2 tablespoons dry white
½ teaspoon salt	wine
⅛ teaspoon white pepper	1 recipe Dee's Clam Sauce
1 teaspoon cornstarch	(recipe on page 175)*

PREPARATION
Peel the garlic cloves and put them through a garlic press, or chop fine. Chop the scallions, keeping the white and green parts separate.

If the shrimp are extra large, split them lengthwise or cut them in half crosswise. Mix with the salt, pepper, and cornstarch. Drain the water chestnuts.

COOKING
Heat the corn oil in a wok over medium-high heat. Add the garlic and scallion whites. When the garlic cooks

* SUBSTITUTIONS
Sea scallops can be used in place of the shrimp. Substitute 2 tablespoons of oyster sauce (see page 29) and 1 tablespoon water for the clam sauce, if you prefer.

to a light brown, add the shrimp. Stir-fry the shrimp until they turn pink. Add the wine and cook 30 seconds. Add the water chestnuts and clam sauce and cook, stirring and turning, until the sauce is hot. Serve topped with the scallion greens as a garnish.

Shrimp with Red Sauce
4 Servings

This is a western Chinese dish. You can make it spicy or reduce the spices to your own taste.

1½ pounds fresh shrimp, cleaned and deveined*	3 garlic cloves
1½ teaspoons salt	1½ teaspoons cornstarch
¼ teaspoon white pepper	3 tablespoons soy sauce
1 tablespoon Tabasco sauce*	¾ cup ground beef or pork
	⅓ cup tomato catsup
1 tablespoon Red Hot sauce*	2 scallions
	6 tablespoons corn oil

PREPARATION

If the shrimp are extra large, cut them in half lengthwise or split them in half crosswise. Mix the shrimp with salt, pepper, and cornstarch.

Mix the ground meat with the soy sauce. Combine the catsup, Tabasco sauce, and Red Hot sauce.

Peel the garlic cloves and put them through a garlic press, or mince with the steel blade.

Chop the scallions, keeping the white and green parts separate.

* SUBSTITUTIONS

Sea scallops are very tasty cooked in this way. You can replace the Tabasco and Red Hot sauce with 2 tablespoons sesame-seed oil with chili (see page 29).

COOKING

Put 3 tablespoons corn oil in a wok over medium-high heat. Add the garlic and scallion whites and cook until they are light brown. Add the shrimp and stir-fry until they turn pink, about 2 or 3 minutes. Add the wine and cook 30 seconds. Remove to a dish and wipe the wok clean with paper towels.

Now heat another 3 tablespoons corn oil in the wok, and when the oil is hot, put in the ground meat. Stir-fry until the meat is brown and cooked through. Add the catsup mixture, return the shrimp to the wok with the sauce, and cook 1 more minute. Serve garnished with the chopped scallion greens.

Stir-Fried Shrimp Shanghai Style
4 Servings

Small freshwater shrimp, like Maine shrimp, were plentiful in the East, so Shanghai style means using small shrimp, or large shrimp cut into small pieces. There is no sauce in this dish.

1½ pounds fresh shrimp, cleaned and deveined	1 scallion
1½ teaspoons salt	¾ cup cooked ham*
⅛ teaspoon white pepper	¾ cup bamboo shoots
1 teaspoon cornstarch	¾ cup green peas, frozen
	¼ cup corn oil

PREPARATION

Soak the shrimp for at least 20 minutes in 2 cups cold water with 1 teaspoon salt added. Drain. Dice large shrimp or use small ones whole. Mix the shrimp with salt, pepper, and cornstarch.

Chop the scallions. Dice the ham and the bamboo shoots (⅜-inch cubes).

* SUBSTITUTION
Smithfield ham will be most tasty.

COOKING

Cook the frozen peas and drain. Heat 1 tablespoon corn oil in the wok and put in the peas and bamboo shoots. Cook, stirring, for about 2 minutes, until they are heated through, then remove. Wipe the wok with paper towels.

Put the remaining 3 tablespoons corn oil in the wok over high heat. Add the scallions. When the scallions are brown, put in the shrimp and stir-fry quickly until they turn pink, about 2 or 3 minutes. Return the vegetables to the wok with the shrimp, add the diced ham, combine well, heat through, and serve.

Deep-Fried Shrimp Balls
   4 Servings

These shrimp balls are so pretty and tasty they are often served as the first course in a banquet dinner. This recipe serves four as a main dish, but if you serve them as an appetizer or first course, there will be enough for eight to ten people.

1 can (8 ounces) water chestnuts	½ teaspoon white pepper
1½ pounds fresh shrimp, cleaned and deveined	1 large egg
	2 tablespoons corn oil
2 scallions	1 small head lettuce
1 teaspoon salt	2 cups corn oil for deep-frying

PROCESSING

Put the water chestnuts in the work bowl with the steel blade and mince by turning the motor on and off quickly 2 or 3 times. Remove the water chestnuts, chop just the white parts of the scallions, and repeat with the shrimp, processing until they are finely chopped.

ADDITIONAL PREPARATION

Mix the shrimp with salt, pepper, beaten egg, scallion whites, water chestnuts, and 2 tablespoons corn oil.

Dip a teaspoon in corn oil and use it to scoop up some of the shrimp mixture. Use the spoon and your fingers to shape balls. Place them on wax paper.

Wash, drain, and shred the lettuce and put it on a serving dish.

COOKING

Heat 2 cups oil to 375 degrees F. Drop the shrimp balls in and deep-fry to a golden brown. (To avoid crowding you may have to fry the balls in two batches.) The shrimp balls will float to the surface when they are done. Drain them on paper towels and place on the lettuce bed.

Serve shrimp balls with a dip or sauce of your choice. Some suggestions: a mixture of equal parts salt and white pepper, sweet-and-sour sauce, or mustard. More authentic sauces would be Hoisin sauce (see page 28), plum sauce, or brown peppercorn-spiced salt.

NOTE

You can freeze the shrimp paste ahead of time and defrost it when you are ready to make the shrimp balls. If you reheat the shrimp balls, they will taste all right but they won't have the puffed-up look.

Shrimp Curry
4 Servings

This is one dish in which large frozen shrimp are acceptable. Cook lots of rice to go with it, and use your judgment about the amount of curry powder and chili your family will like.

1 medium carrot
2 medium onions
2 green peppers
1½ pounds fresh or frozen
    shrimp, cleaned and
    deveined*
½ teaspoon salt
1 teaspoon dry white wine

1¾ teaspoons cornstarch
¾ cup chicken broth
3 tablespoons curry
    powder*
1 tablespoon water
¼ cup corn oil
1 teaspoon sugar
1 teaspoon chili powder
    (optional)

PROCESSING

Scrape the carrot and cut into lengths to fit the feed tube. With the slicing disk in place, process to get thin slices.

ADDITIONAL PREPARATION

Peel the onions and cut crosswise in half, then cut each half in quarters. Cut the green peppers in 1-inch-square pieces.

Mix the shrimp with salt, wine and 1 teaspoon cornstarch.

Mix the chicken broth with the remaining ¾ teaspoons cornstarch.

Mix the curry powder with 1 tablespoon water to make a paste.

COOKING

Put 1 tablespoon corn oil in a saucepan and sauté the onion until it turns light brown. Add the green peppers and carrots and cook 30 seconds. Add the chicken-broth mixture and cook until the sauce thickens. Set it aside.

Put the remaining 3 tablespoons corn oil in a wok or pan and set over high heat. When the oil is hot, put in

* SUBSTITUTIONS

Scallops are a delicious substitute for the shrimp. Sun-brand curry paste will give a special flavor. Use it instead of the curry powder and the tablespoon of water.

the shrimp and stir-fry until they turn pink, about 2 or 3 minutes. Remove the shrimp with a slotted spoon.

Put the curry paste into the wok and cook until it becomes a little darker in color. Return the shrimp to the wok with the paste and stir to coat. Add sugar and chili powder. Pour in the sauce with the vegetables, combine well, and cook 1 minute. Serve hot with plain rice.

NOTE

This dish reheats well because there is ample sauce. Do not reheat in the oven; just quickly heat in a pan or wok.

9
Duck Main Dishes

If you shy away from serving duck because it has more fat than chicken, these recipes will convince you that duck doesn't have to be fatty. The two cooking methods described here remove most of the fat and give you skin that is crisp, meat that is deliciously moist. True, these methods do take time, but I think you will agree that the results are worth it.

The Famous Peking Duck
4 to 6 Servings

This is actually a recipe for roast duck, but the way it is prepared and served originated in Peking, so it has taken its name from that city. In traditional Chinese cookbooks many, many pages were devoted to instructions for raising and feeding ducks, and even on how to build an oven to roast them. There were restaurants that specialized in Peking Duck. It was the only main course they served; the rest of the menu consisted of side dishes designed to go with the duck. In this country most restaurants require two days' advance notice to serve Peking Duck, so you mustn't forget to call ahead.

The preparation of the duck isn't complicated, but the proper drying time is critical. The traditional method is to hang the duck to dry, then give it a "bath," then hang to dry the skin again. The duck is suspended in the oven to roast, so the entire skin becomes crisp. Peking Duck is eaten with a special sauce dabbed on with scallion "brushes" and rolled up in a steamed pancake. It's quite a production, and most Chinese banquets would not be complete without Peking Duck as one of the main attractions. I have devised a simplified method of preparing this dish that retains the authentic flavor and the traditional method of serving.

1 duck, 5 pounds or over, fresh or frozen	½ cup cold water
1 tablespoon white vinegar	Dee's Duck Sauce (recipe page 139)
3 tablespoons honey	12 Mandarin Pancakes (recipe page 140)
13 scallion stalks	
3 tablespoons cornstarch	

PREPARATION—2 DAYS AHEAD

Wash the duck thoroughly under cool running water, making sure the cavity is clean. Pat dry with paper towels. Cut off the tail end and cut the wing tips off at the first joint. Use four wooden skewers, 4 inches long, to hold the legs and wings away from the body. (The duck will look as though it had 4 stretched-out legs.) This allows air to get to all parts of the skin and dry it thoroughly. Place the duck on a large cake rack or on the rack of a roasting pan and leave it in the bottom of the refrigerator overnight, uncovered.

PREPARATION—1 DAY AHEAD

The next day, bring 6 cups of water to boil in a large pot or wok with the vinegar, honey, and 1 cut-up scallion stalk. Mix the cornstarch with ½ cup cold water and add gradually to thicken the boiling liquid. Now submerge the whole duck in the boiling mixture for 1 minute. If the pot isn't big enough, dunk the duck one end at a time. When the duck is well coated, put it back on the cake rack and again let it stand in the refrigerator for at least 24 hours. The skin will feel dry to the touch when the duck is ready for the next step. Meanwhile, you can prepare the Scallion Brushes, Dee's Duck Sauce, and Mandarin Pancakes.

To make Scallion Brushes: Cut scallions 3 inches from the white bulb and discard the green leafy part (or save to garnish other dishes). Cut off the tip of the root end. Using a very sharp knife, cut the scallions halfway down from the green end. The first cut will split the green part in half. Then make another cut across the first one to slit the scallion into quarters. Two more cuts will make eighths. Be sure each time to cut only halfway down. Submerge the 12 scallions in ice water and let them stand in the refrigerator. The green ends of each scallion will open up like a brush with the white bulb as the handle.

To make Dee's Duck Sauce, follow the recipe on page 139.

To make the Mandarin Pancakes, follow the recipe on page 140. You can do them ahead and keep them in the refrigerator for a few days, wrapped in aluminum foil, or even freeze them. Remember to start steaming the pancakes about 30 minutes before you are ready to serve the duck.

COOKING

When the duck is dry and ready for roasting, preheat the oven to 350 degrees F. Lightly grease an oven rack and set it in the middle of the oven. Fill a shallow 11- by 14-inch pan with water, about three quarters full, and place it on a second oven rack so that the top of the pan is about 2 inches below the first rack. While the duck roasts, this pan will collect the fat that drips off, and the water will keep it from smoking. When the oven reaches 350 degrees F., place the duck breast side up on the greased rack. Roast for 30 minutes. Turn the duck breast side down and roast for 45 minutes. Finally, turn the duck breast side up again and roast for another 30 minutes.

When the duck has cooled enough to handle, remove the skewers and use a sharp knife to disjoint the wings and drumsticks. Carefully remove all the skin from the rest of the meat and cut it in pieces about 2 inches square. Remove all the duck meat and cut it into 2-inch slices, making them as uniform as possible.

To serve, place the duck meat in the center of a platter and arrange the pieces of skin, the drumsticks, and the wings around the edge of the platter. Serve the duck sauce* on a luncheon plate with the Scallion Brushes around the edge. A dinner plate can hold the stack of steamed Mandarin Pancakes.

To eat Peking Duck, put a piece of skin and some meat on a pancake, dip a Scallion Brush in the sauce and dab it on the duck, then roll up the duck and the scallion in the pancake and eat it like a sandwich.

* SUBSTITUTION

If Hoisin sauce (see page 28) is available, you can make an alternate dip for the duck by combining ½ cup Hoisin sauce, 2 tablespoons sugar, 1 tablespoon water, and 1 teaspoon sesame-seed oil.

Dee's Duck Sauce

2 tablespoons smooth peanut butter	Dash garlic powder
4 tablespoons soy sauce	6 drops Red Hot sauce (more if you like)
2 tablespoons honey	Dash salt
2 tablespoons white vinegar	Dash white pepper

Combine all ingredients in a glass jar and mix well. This sauce will keep for a week in the refrigerator.

Mandarin Pancakes

The name for these pancakes in Mandarin is *b' ou bin,* which means "thin crepe," and that is exactly what they are. Yet the texture is quite different from crepes served here, and in fact I have not been able to duplicate them with an electric crepe maker. They require some skill and patience, yet all of my students have made them successfully at the first try. My three sons are crazy about them, and I once made 36 pancakes for them in 40 minutes as a snack. So you see it isn't that difficult.

1 cup all-purpose flour, unsifted	⅓ cup boiling water
1 teaspoon salt	2 tablespoons corn oil

Put the flour and salt in the work bowl with the steel blade. Turn on the motor and pour the boiling water in a slow stream through the feed tube. Process only until the dough looks mealy, like oatmeal. Turn the dough out onto a board and knead until smooth, about 2 or 3 minutes. Add a little flour only if necessary. The dough should be dry to the touch but not stiff.

Divide the dough into 12 little balls and roll out each ball to a flat disk about 2½ inches in diameter. Brush corn oil on six of the disks and cover each with one of the ungreased disks. You will now have 6 double rounds of dough. Press the edges together and roll out each double disk to a thin pancake about 5½ to 6 inches in diameter. Turn the disks frequently as you roll to maintain a round shape. If necessary, dust the pancakes lightly with flour as you roll, but do not use too much flour or the pancakes will become stiff. (I have found that the Foley pastry frame with the canvas pastry cloth and rolling-pin "stocking" is helpful because it enables you to use less flour.)

Set an ungreased flat-bottomed pan, at least 8 inches in diameter, over low heat. When the pan is hot, put in one double pancake. Turn the pancake when bubbles appear between the two layers of dough and the dough starts to turn beige. Cook the other side for 30 seconds. Remove from the pan and separate the two pancakes with a pointed knife. The seams where the pancakes are joined will become visible during cooking, so you will be able to see where to slide the knife.

Cook and separate each pair of pancakes, for a total of 12.* Stack each pair with the cooked sides together to prevent sticking, wrap in aluminum foil, and refrigerate or freeze until ready to use.

Steam the pancakes just before serving. They can be served flat in a stack, folded in half or in quarters. Mandarin Pancakes can be made ahead and stored in the freezer wrapped in foil. Make a big batch when you have the time and freeze them in stacks of 12.

Crispy Duck
4 to 6 Servings

This is a second cousin to Peking Duck, almost as tasty and requiring less time to prepare. You season, steam, and then broil the duck. Although the traditional recipe calls for deep-fat frying, broiling is less messy and also lower in calories. The duck will be just as crisp and flavorful.

* SUBSTITUTION

Unbaked soft rolls, from your own recipe or the supermarket, can be steamed for 10 minutes and served as a substitute for Mandarin Pancakes.

1 duck, 5 pounds or over, fresh or frozen	⅛ teaspoon ground ginger*
2 tablespoons peppercorns*	1 scallion
3 tablespoons kosher salt*	1 tablespoon soy sauce
1 teaspoon white pepper	12 steamed rolls*
¼ teaspoon nutmeg	Dee's Duck Sauce (see page 139)

PREPARATION—1 DAY AHEAD

Wash the duck thoroughly under cool running water, making sure the cavity is clean, and cut off the tail end. Put peppercorns and salt in a small pan and cook 5 minutes over medium heat, stirring occasionally. Add white pepper, nutmeg, and ginger, and mix well. Rub this spice mixture all over the duck, inside and out. Put the scallion stalk in the cavity.

Refrigerate the spiced duck in a plastic bag, tightly closed, for at least 24 hours. This will allow the seasonings and spices to penetrate and flavor the duck meat.

COOKING

The duck is now ready for steaming. Place it on the longest-legged rack you have, inside a turkey roaster or a very large pot. Fill the pot with water just below the level of the rack. Cover the pot and steam over high heat for 1½ hours. While the duck is cooking, the fat will drip into the water. Check the water level often and add more boiling water as it evaporates.

After the duck has been steamed, remove to a rack

* SUBSTITUTIONS

Use Sze-Chuan peppercorns instead of black ones if they are available (see page 30). If kosher salt is not available, use regular salt instead. Also, if you can obtain fresh ginger root (see page 27), eliminate the ground ginger, cut a large slice of the fresh root, and place it in the cavity of the duck with the scallion.

For steamed rolls, start with unbaked rolls from the supermarket or use your own recipe. Instead of baking, steam the rolls on a rack over boiling water in a covered pan for ten minutes. After steaming you can refrigerate or freeze the rolls for future use.

to cool. Crispy Duck can be made ahead up to this point and refrigerated for 2 or 3 days, or can even be frozen until needed and then defrosted. When ready to serve, brush with soy sauce. Use a cleaver to cut the duck in half and separate the wings and drumsticks from the body. Arrange the pieces on aluminum foil in a broiling pan with skin side up and broil 2 inches from the flame until brown and crisp. (In summer this step can be done over the barbeque coals, if you prefer.)

Serve immediately. Put duck halves, wings, and legs in the center of a large platter. Arrange steamed rolls (see below) around the edge and serve sauce on the side in a small dish. To eat, cut off a piece of meat with skin, place in a roll, spoon on some sauce, and eat with your fingers like a sandwich.

10
Vegetables

Vegetables excite me because nature provides us with good nourishment in such a delightful variety of forms. I prefer to see each vegetable cooked by itself, to maintain its unique texture and individuality. I will show you the method of cooking and the best way to cut each vegetable so that it will look most appealing. But the final decision about cooking time is up to you, because each person's preference is different. With a little tasting and experience, you will quickly determine the degree of crispness or softness you prefer.

When you buy vegetables, make sure the leaves are not dried up or blemished. Stems should be crisp, not flabby, so you know that if you cut them with a knife, juice will flow out. Squash must be firm to the touch.

Since leafy vegetables will rot from too much moisture, the best way to store them is unwashed, rolled up tight in a paper bag, and then enclosed in a plastic bag. Other vegetables can be stored in the same way, and you will be able to keep them up to 5 days or even a week in the vegetable bin. But do try to cook and eat all vegetables as soon as possible, because every day that you store them they lose vitamins and flavor.

Since I have found that more and more people prefer to cut down on the amount of salt they eat, I have kept my recipes on the lightly salted side. You can add more salt if you prefer, but please taste first to see if you really want it.

Green Beans Sze-Chuan
4 Servings

This recipe originated in the Sze-Chuan province of western China. The method of deep-frying first and then cooking the beans with a sauce gives them an unusual texture that is out of this world.

1½ pounds fresh green beans	1 tablespoon sugar
	1 tablespoon cider vinegar
2½ tablespoons soy sauce	¼ cup chicken broth
¼ cup ground beef	3 cups corn oil
1 small onion	½ teaspoon crushed red
4 scallions	peppers (optional)

PREPARATION
Wash the green beans and cut into 2-inch pieces. Dry thoroughly on paper towels, making sure no moisture remains. Add ½ tablespoon of the soy sauce to the ground beef. Chop the onion with steel blade in food processor. Chop the scallion greens and whites separately. Combine sugar, vinegar, and 2 tablespoons soy sauce with the chicken broth.

COOKING
Heat 3 cups of corn oil in a wok or large frying pan. Drop in the green beans and deep-fry until their skins look wrinkled. With a slotted spoon remove the beans to a dish. Pour the oil into a heat-proof bowl. Return 3 tablespoons of the oil to the wok over medium-

high heat. (Store the rest of the oil; it can be used repeatedly for deep-frying.)

Put the scallion whites into the wok and stir-fry 1 minute. Add the onions and beef and stir-fry one more minute. Add the chicken-broth mixture and bring to a boil. Now add the fried beans. Stir and cook until the liquid is absorbed. At this point, if you like spicy-hot food, add the crushed peppers, stir, and cook a few seconds longer.

Serve garnished with chopped scallion greens.

Authentic Version

To make the truly Chinese version of this dish, you will need dried shrimp (see page 27) and Sze-Chuan mustard pickles. A quarter cup of each takes the place of the ground beef and the onion. Soak the dried shrimp in a little sherry for an hour. Mince the shrimp and the mustard pickles, add to the scallions, and continue cooking as directed in the basic recipes. These two ingredients add a spicy, sharp flavor to the dish.

A Tip for Easy Cooking
Deep-fry the beans in a small electric fryer for 5 minutes. This leaves the wok free for stir-frying. You can make this dish in no time at all.

Spicy Eggplant
4 Servings

The original recipe for this dish, which comes from the western region, calls for deep-frying. I suggest stir-frying instead, since in this way the eggplant absorbs less oil. However, I have also included the authentic recipe.

2 scallions	⅓ cup chicken broth
4 garlic cloves	⅓ cup corn oil
2 medium eggplants	½ teaspoon crushed red
2 tablespoons soy sauce	peppers (optional)
1 teaspoon sugar	¼ teaspoon powdered
2 tablespoons cider vinegar	ginger

PROCESSING

Cut scallions, both white and usable green parts, into 1½-inch lengths. Process with the steel blade, turning the machine on and off 2 or 3 times. Remove from the work bowl, replace the steel blade, and chop the garlic. This should take only about 3 seconds. Set aside the scallions and garlic in separate dishes.

ADDITIONAL PREPARATION

Peel the eggplants and cut into ½-inch slices, then into strips ½ inch wide and 2 inches long. Dry thoroughly on paper towels, to make sure no moisture remains. Combine the soy sauce, sugar, vinegar, and chicken broth, and set aside.

COOKING

Heat the corn oil in a wok or frying pan. Add the chopped garlic and, if you like a spicy-hot flavor, the red peppers. Cook until the garlic turns light brown. Add the eggplant and cook, stirring and turning, until it is soft, about 10 to 15 minutes. Add the liquid mixture and bring to a boil. Add the ginger and continue boiling until the liquid is almost completely absorbed. Serve garnished with the chopped scallions.

Authentic Version

2 scallions
4 garlic cloves
½-inch slice of fresh ginger
   root (or enough to make
   1 tablespoon, chopped)
2 medium eggplants
2 tablespoons soy sauce
1 teaspoon sugar

2 tablespoons brown
   vinegar (see page 26)
⅓ cup chicken broth
3 cups corn oil
1 tablespoon hot Sze-Chuan
   bean sauce (see page 30)
1 tablespoon sesame-seed
   oil (see page 29)

PROCESSING

Chop scallions and garlic as described in the stir-fry version, above. Chop ginger root in the same way.

ADDITIONAL PREPARATION

Peel and slice eggplant as above. Combine the soy sauce, sugar, vinegar, and chicken broth, and set aside.

COOKING

Heat the corn oil in a wok or large frying pan. Drop in the eggplant slices and deep-fry until soft. With a slotted spoon remove the eggplant to a dish. Put the oil into a heat-proof bowl. Return 2 tablespoons of the oil to the wok over medium-high heat. (Store the rest of the oil; it can be used repeatedly for deep-frying.)

Add the garlic, ginger, and hot bean paste to the wok. Stir a few minutes. Add the liquid mixture and bring to a boil. Add the fried eggplant and cook until the sauce is absorbed. To serve, sprinkle with the sesame-seed oil and the chopped scallions.

Cucumbers Eastern Style
   4 Servings

Most people have never tasted cooked cucumbers, but once they try it, they usually like it. Cucumbers should be cooked until they are soft, to lose their raw taste completely. This dish is a favorite in the eastern region of China.

½ cup shrimp, fresh or frozen, cleaned and deveined	3 tablespoons corn oil
	¼ cup chicken broth
	Salt to taste (optional)
4 medium cucumbers	

PROCESSING
Chop shrimp with the steel blade, turning the motor on and off 2 or 3 times.

ADDITIONAL PREPARATION
Peel the cucumbers, quarter lengthwise, and remove the seeds. Split each piece in half lengthwise and cut into 2-inch-long pieces.

COOKING
Heat the oil in a wok or frying pan. Add the cucumbers and cook, stirring and turning occasionally, for 10 to 15 minutes. The cucumber pieces will become translucent. Add the chopped shrimp and continue stirring and tossing until they become pink. Add the chicken broth and simmer 5 minutes. Season with salt to taste, if necessary, and serve. This dish reheats nicely, so you can make it ahead.

Authentic Version

To the Chinese, the flavor of dried shrimp (see page 27) adds a great deal to this dish. Substitute ¼ cup, soaked in a little sherry, for the fresh chopped shrimp.

Stir-Fried Cabbage
    4 Servings

When I was young, there was a newspaper cartoon strip called "Bringing Up Father." Every time the husband wanted corned beef and cabbage, he had a fight with his wife because she hated the smell. It's true—when cabbage is cooked for a long time, it gives out a very strong odor that many people object to. But when you stir-fry cabbage this way, it cooks so quickly that the cabbage has no chance to release its odor. The result is crisp and delicious.

2- to 3-pound head of cabbage	¼ cup corn oil
1 carrot	1 teaspoon salt
2 scallions	⅓ cup chicken broth
	2 teaspoons soy sauce

PROCESSING

Discard any damaged outer leaves of cabbage. Cut the cabbage in quarters and core. Cut the quarters lengthwise into halves or thirds to fit the feed tube. With the slicing disk in place, stand the cabbage wedges on end and process. The result will be nicely shredded cabbage. Set the cabbage aside, and without washing the work bowl replace the slicing disk with the shredding disk. Scrape the carrot with a vegetable parer and cut it crosswise into 2-inch pieces to fit the width of the feed tube. Place them in the tube lying down, one on top of the other. Process with steady pressure to get long shreds of carrot.

ADDITIONAL PREPARATION

Cut off the white parts of the scallions and save them for use in another recipe. Cut the green parts into 2-inch pieces.

COOKING

Heat the oil in a wok or pan. Add the salt, then put in the shredded cabbage all at once and stir-fry for 1 minute. Add the carrot shreds and scallions, then the chicken broth. Cook, stirring and tossing, for another minute. Stir in the soy sauce and serve.

Crunchy Broccoli
4 Servings

Broccoli is usually available the year round, and I like it so much I serve it once a week at least.

1 bunch fresh broccoli	½ teaspoon salt
¼ cup corn oil	¼ cup water

PROCESSING
Cut the broccoli head into bite-size flowerets. Wash and dry the flowerets and the stems. With a sharp paring knife (not a swivel-type one) peel off the outer layers of the stems. Check to make sure all the stringy white fibers are removed. Cut the stems in 2-inch-long pieces and lay them one on top of the other in the feed tube. Use the slicing disk and process with pressure.

COOKING
Put oil in the wok or pan over medium high heat. When the oil is hot, add the salt and then the broccoli stems and flowerets. Stir-fry until the broccoli turns a darker green. Quickly add the water. The steam will help to cook and tenderize the broccoli. If you like your vegetables crunchy, just a few additional tossings will be enough. Remove the broccoli with a slotted spoon and serve.

Tasty Cauliflower
4 Servings

Many of my students tell me their families won't eat cauliflower, but when they learn how to make this dish and try it out at home, they come back with a different story. It makes me happy.

1 large carrot	½ cup chicken broth
1 small or half a large head of cauliflower	2 teaspoons salt
1 teaspoon cornstarch	¼ cup corn oil

PROCESSING
Scrape the carrot and cut it into 2½-inch pieces to fit the feed tube. With the slicing disk in place, pack the tube with the carrot pieces, standing up. Process with light pressure to get very thin carrot slices.

ADDITIONAL PREPARATION
Break cauliflower into bite-size pieces, cutting flowerets in half when necessary.

Mix cornstarch and chicken broth.

COOKING
Bring 4 cups water with 1½ teaspoons salt to a boil in a large pot. Add the cauliflower pieces. When the water returns to a boil, remove the cauliflower to a strainer, run under cold tap water, and drain. Heat the oil in a wok or pan over medium-high heat. When the oil is hot, add the remaining ½ teaspoon salt with the cauliflower. Stir and turn for a few seconds to coat with oil, then add the carrots. Stir and cook about 2 minutes. Stir the broth mixture and pour it over the cauliflower. Cook, stirring, about 1 minute more. Remove from the wok and serve immediately.

Wonderful Chinese Celery Cabbage
4 Servings

There are two kinds of Chinese cabbage. One variety, celery cabbage, is longer, with smooth leaves. The other is shorter and rounder, with slightly curly leaves. This is sometimes called Napa Cabbage, from the California Napa Valley, where it is grown. The shorter variety is a little more tender and tasty, but they are both wonderful vegetables, full of vitamins and low in calories. You can easily grow them in your own garden, if you want to eat them at the peak of freshness.

2 to 3 pounds Chinese
  cabbage
¼ cup corn oil
1 teaspoon salt
⅓ cup chicken broth

PREPARATION

Wash the cabbage and pat dry with paper towels. Cut the leafy parts from the stem parts and separate them into 2 piles. Cut the leafy parts into large pieces, about 4 inches long. Cut the stem parts into long strips, 2 inches by ½ inch.

COOKING

Heat the oil in a wok or pan. Add salt. Put in the stem slices and stir-fry for 1 minute. Add the leafy parts and cook and stir until the leaves are soft. Add the chicken broth and bring it to a boil. Simmer 1 minute and serve immediately. If you prefer vegetables on the soft side, you can simmer the leaves a little longer. You can also cook this dish in advance and reheat it.

How to Make Bean Curd
and Use It

There are many vegetarians in China, and they are very dependent on soybeans for their protein. As a result, soybean products come in many varieties. The most famous of them is bean curd. Made by curdling soybean milk, bean curd is white and comes in cakelike pieces about 3 or 4 inches square. The consistency can vary greatly, from soft, somewhat like a hard custard, to firm, like stale bread. You will see many kinds of bean curds in Chinese markets. Because the Japanese prefer soft bean curd, this is the only type that is usually available in Japanese markets.

Bean curd will keep in your refrigerator for about a week if you cover it with water and change the water daily. In warm weather it spoils quite easily. If you freeze bean curd, the water content freezes separately, and after defrosting the bean curd looks like a piece of sponge. Some cooks prefer it this way.

It's not easy to make bean curd, and commercial makers keep their recipes a dark secret. Japanese markets do sell packages of soybean powder with instructions on how to turn it into bean curd. The result is not great, but passable. If you cannot find prepared bean curd, or simply want to face the challenge of making it yourself from scratch, here's how.

1 cup dry soybeans	**1 tablespoon calcium sulfate (plaster of Paris)**

Also have on hand:

Cheesecloth	A loaf cake pan or
A heavy cloth bag (linen or	8-by8-inch cake pan
unbleached muslin)	

PROCESSING

Soak soybeans overnight in water to cover; drain, and rinse.

With the steel blade in place, put two cups of water in the work bowl with half the soybeans and liquefy. Repeat with the other half.

ADDITIONAL PREPARATION

Pour the liquid mixture into the bag and hold it over a large bowl, twisting the top of the bag to squeeze out as much as possible of the soybean milk. You should get about 4 cups of liquid. If not, put the residue in the bag back in the processor, add more water, and process again. Repeat by straining through the bag again.

COOKING

Measure 3 cups soybean milk and bring it to a boil in a saucepan. Mix the calcium sulfate with the remaining cup of cold soybean milk. Turn off the heat and pour the cold mixture into the boiling milk. Stir and mix very quickly. Pour into a square or rectangular pan. In about an hour the soybean milk will curdle and become bean curd.

Fold three or four layers of cheesecloth. Unmold the bean curd, place it on the folded cheesecloth, and wrap it up. Excess liquid will seep out and make the bean curd firmer. You can even put a weight on the wrapped bean curd to press out more liquid, for a still firmer cake.

When the curd is the consistency you like, cut it into 2-inch or 3-inch squares. Cover them with cold water and store in the refrigerator. If you change the water every day, the bean curd cakes should keep up to a week.

Using Bean Curd Cakes in Recipes

Allow about 1 cake (up to 3 inches square) for each person. Cut in slices, cubes, or strips to match the other ingredients in the recipe and add to the dish along with the sauce or gravy. It will be ready to eat after 2 minutes of cooking.

How to Grow Bean Sprouts and Use Them

Sprouting your own bean sprouts is the easiest indoor gardening you can do, and very gratifying. From only 1¾ ounces of mung beans you get 1¼ pounds of beautiful bean sprouts. Once you do it, you will probably never again buy bean sprouts from the market.

Also have on hand:

⅓ cup (1¾ ounces) dry mung beans

An empty 46-ounce juice can, with its severed lid intact

A clean dish towel

Soak the dry mung beans overnight in water to cover. Rinse and drain. Punch 4 holes in the bottom of the can with a beer-can opener. Put the severed lid on it to cover the holes and keep the beans from escaping. Put the soaked beans in the can and cover with the towel, folded in layers to fit. Run cold water over the towel and let the water drain off. Do this thoroughly at least 4 times a day.

By the fourth or fifth day the beans should have sprouted to 5 or 6 times their volume. If the weather is warm, 5 days will be enough. In winter the beans may take 7 days to sprout fully. The bean sprouts you get will be long and straight, pure white in color, and rich in vitamin B.

Bean sprouts will stay fresh for a few days, stored in a plastic bag in the refrigerator. Before I use them, I like to pick off the stringy parts. Bean sprouts can be added raw to salads, or stir-fried to serve with any other dish.

Stir-Fried Bean Sprouts
4 Servings

3 tablespoons corn oil	1 teaspoon salt
1 pound fresh bean sprouts	3 scallions, chopped

Heat oil in a wok or frying pan until almost smoky. Add all the bean sprouts at once. Stir and turn quickly. Sprinkle with salt and continue stir-frying for 1 minute. The sprouts give up liquid, so remove with a slotted spoon. Garnish with chopped scallions and serve as a side dish.

Asparagus
4 Servings

The beauty of this dish is the texture, and the trick is in the cutting. You must use fresh asparagus.

1 can (8 ounces) water
  chestnuts
3 pounds fresh asparagus

3 tablespoons corn oil
1 teaspoon salt

PROCESSING

With the slicing disk in place, pack the feed tube with water chestnuts and process with medium pressure.

ADDITIONAL PREPARATION

Wash the asparagus and drain on paper towels. Discard the tough white parts. Cut the asparagus stalks by holding a sharp knife at a 45-degree angle and making ¼-inch slices.

COOKING

Heat the corn oil in a wok or frying pan over medium-high heat. Add salt and the asparagus slices. Stir-fry for about 2 minutes, until the asparagus turns a darker green. Add the water chestnuts and stir-fry for another minute. Remove with a slotted spoon and serve immediately.

Spinach
  4 Servings

Fresh spinach is almost a different vegetable from the frozen variety. And with stir-frying it becomes even more tasty. Try it and see.

½ cup bamboo shoots
2 pounds fresh spinach
3 tablespoons corn oil

1 teaspoon salt
Pinch of sugar
1 teaspoon soy sauce

PROCESSING

With the shredding disk in place, pack the feed tube with bamboo shoots and process with medium pressure to shred.

ADDITIONAL PREPARATION

Wash spinach thoroughly. If spinach comes in plants instead of loose in packages, it isn't necessary to separate the leaves. The reddish root part is very sweet.

COOKING

Heat corn oil in a wok or pan over medium-high heat. Add salt and then all the spinach. Turn while cooking until the spinach is soft. Add bamboo shoots and mix well. Lower the heat, cover, and simmer for 2 or 3 minutes. The spinach gives out its own liquid. Remove from heat, sprinkle with sugar, and add the soy sauce. Mix well and serve.

Turnips
4 Servings

This method of cooking turnips eliminates most of their strong cooking odor, and it also turns them into a tasty and interesting dish.

2 to 3 pounds turnips	¼ cup hot water
2 cloves garlic	2 scallions
2 chicken-bouillon cubes	3 tablespoons corn oil

PROCESSING

Peel the turnips and cut into large chunks that will fit sideways into the feed tube. With the slicing disk in place put a turnip chunk in the feed tube and process with firm pressure for thick slices. Now place the slices side by side on edge in the tube and process again. You will get matchstick pieces like thin French fries. Repeat until all of the turnips have been cut in this manner. (If you have a French-fry cutting disk for your machine, you can put it to good use in this recipe.)

ADDITIONAL PREPARATION

Peel the garlic cloves and put them through a garlic press. Dissolve the chicken-bouillon cubes in the water.

Chop the scallions, both white and usable green parts.

COOKING

Bring 6 cups of water to a boil in a large pot, add the turnips, and boil 3 minutes. Pour off all the water and drain the turnips. Heat the oil in a wok or pan. Put in the blanched turnips, stirring and turning for a few seconds. Add the minced garlic and cook, stirring, about 3 more minutes. Add the bouillon and the scallions. Bring to a boil and simmer for a few minutes, stirring occasionally, until some of the liquid evaporates.

Celery
   4 Servings

By cutting celery stalks into thin slices, you can stir-fry it briefly and enjoy a crisp vegetable.

1 celery plant	⅓ cup chicken broth
1 carrot	3 tablespoons corn oil
½ teaspoon cornstarch	½ teaspoon salt

PREPARATION

Cut off the stem end and the leafy parts of the celery. Separate the stalk, wash and drain. Pull off the stringy fibers. Cut each stalk into thin slices by placing the knife at a 45-degree angle.

Scrape the carrot and cut at a 45-degree angle to make thin slices. You will get oval slices instead of round ones.

Combine the cornstarch and chicken broth in a small dish.

COOKING

Heat corn oil in a wok or pan over medium-high heat. Add the salt and then the celery slices. Stir-fry for one minute. Add the carrot slices and stir-fry 1 minute more. Stir the cornstarch and broth to mix well and pour over the vegetables. Bring to a boil, stirring constantly. When the sauce has thickened and the vegetables look glossy, they are ready to serve.

Watercress
4 Servings

I bet you've never eaten cooked watercress. After you try it, you will want to serve it often. Chinese chefs love to use it as a garnish for special dishes because it is so green and pretty.

2 bunches watercress
2 teaspoons salt
2 tablespoons corn oil

2 tablespoons roasted pine nuts (optional)

PREPARATION
Wash and drain watercress.

COOKING
Bring 4 cups of water to a boil. Add 1½ teaspoons salt. Drop the watercress in for 10 seconds and lift out. Heat the oil in a wok or pan over medium-high heat. Add the remaining ½ teaspoon salt and the watercress and stir-fry for 1 minute. Serve immediately, sprinkled with pine nuts.

Lettuce
4 Servings

My family loves hearts of lettuce as salad. What do I do with the outer leaves? I usually stir-fry and serve them as a vegetable. Of course, if you stir-fry the whole lettuce, it is even better.

1 head lettuce
3 tablespoons corn oil
2 cloves garlic
1 teaspoon salt

1 teaspoon oyster sauce
(optional, see page 29)
1 tablespoon sesame seeds

PREPARATION
Separate the lettuce leaves. Wash, drain, and dry with paper towels.

COOKING
Heat the corn oil in a wok or pan over medium-high heat. Put the garlic cloves through a garlic press and add to the oil. Add the salt and lettuce leaves and stir-fry for 3 minutes. Add oyster sauce, sprinkle with sesame seeds, and serve.

Zucchini
4 Servings

Nothing tastes better than fresh young zucchini, especially from your own garden. Be sure to eat it while it is small. Last year we overlooked one in our garden, and it grew to 22 inches. We ate it anyway, but it was far less tasty than the small ones. Cook zucchini with or without the green skin, according to your own preference. I like to roll-cut zucchini; it makes a prettier dish.

1 thick slice ham (boiled or
Virginia)
4 zucchini, about 8 or 9
inches long

3 tablespoons corn oil
⅓ cup chicken broth
Salt to taste

PROCESSING
Cut the ham slice in quarters and put in the work bowl with the steel blade. Mince by turning the motor on and off quickly 2 or 3 times.

ADDITIONAL PREPARATION

Wash and roll-cut zucchini (see sketch on page 32), with or without skin.

COOKING

Heat the oil in a wok or pan. When it is almost smoking, put in the zucchini pieces. Stir and turn 2 minutes. Add chicken broth and simmer 3 to 5 minutes, to the tenderness you prefer. Remove to a serving dish and serve sprinkled with minced ham.

11
Noodles

To the Chinese, noodles are a symbol of longevity, so they are always served on birthdays. The longer the noodle strands, the better! But since everybody loves them, they may also turn up on any day throughout the year, and not just as a luncheon or dinner dish. Chinese people also enjoy noodles for breakfast or as a light snack, served hot or cold, and there are delicious soups with noodles that can be a whole meal in themselves.

With a food processor and a noodle machine, you can produce your own fresh noodles almost effortlessly. I make them in big batches and freeze them to use as needed, and I will tell you how. I will also tell you how to mix the dough and make the noodles by hand—not really as formidable as it sounds. And of course you can use commercial noodles and pasta as well in all of the recipes that follow, choosing from the dazzling variety in Chinese, Italian, and American markets.

Plain Noodles
  2 to 4 Servings

MIXING DOUGH WITH THE FOOD PROCESSOR

1½ cups flour   ⅓ cup plus 1 tablespoon
½ teaspoon salt   water

With the steel blade in place, put the flour and salt
in the work bowl. Cover and keep the machine working
as you pour water in a slow, steady stream through the
feed tube. The mixture will become meal-like and then
form into a solid mass in about 30 to 40 seconds. Remove
the dough, press it into a compact ball, and wrap closely
in aluminum foil. Refrigerate for several hours or overnight.

MIXING DOUGH BY HAND

1½ cups flour   ½ cup lukewarm water
½ teaspoons salt

Mix flour and salt and add the water gradually to
form a smooth dough. Turn out on a floured board and
knead in additional flour, as necessary, until the dough
loses its stickiness. Wrap the dough closely in aluminum
foil and refrigerate for several hours or overnight.

MAKING NOODLES WITH A PASTA MACHINE
Put the dough through the machine once at the
widest setting. Then reset to the thinnest setting and put
the dough through again. Select the noodle width you prefer and put the dough through the machine. Freeze
noodles in plastic bags.

FORMING NOODLES BY HAND
Roll out the dough on a floured board to a
thickness of $\frac{1}{16}$ inch. Fold or roll up the sheet of dough

and cut it with a sharp knife into the width you prefer. Freeze noodles in plastic bags.

Egg Noodles
2 to 4 Servings

1½ cups flour   ⅓ cup water
½ teaspoon salt   1 egg yolk

PROCESSING
With the steel blade in place, put flour and salt in the work bowl. Beat the egg yolk and add it to the water. Cover and keep the machine working as you pour the liquid in a slow, steady stream through the feed tube. The dough will become meal-like and then form into a solid mass in about 30 to 40 seconds. Remove the dough, press it into a compact ball, and wrap closely in aluminum foil. Refrigerate for several hours or overnight.

NOTE
See preceding recipe for Plain Noodles for instructions on mixing dough by hand, and for cutting noodles by hand or with a pasta machine.

Mrs. Wang's Lau Mien, or Tossed Noodles
4 to 6 Servings

Lau means "mix" and *mien* means "noodles." So Lau Mien, which you see often on menus in Chinese restaurants, is a dish of noodles mixed with all sorts of good things. It is very popular in the southern Chinese cuisine. The combination I have devised is most tasty and also substantial enough to be a main dish.

1 small head cabbage
1 can (8 ounces) sliced
    bamboo shoots
¼ pound fresh shrimp,
    cleaned, deveined, and
    partially frozen
2 scallions
½ pound fresh mushrooms*
1 pound fresh egg noodles
    or packaged vermicelli

½ pound lean pork
    tenderloin, partially
    frozen
¼ teaspoon salt
1½ teaspoons cornstarch
5 tablespoons soy sauce
⅓ cup corn oil
1 egg

PROCESSING

Remove the outer leaves of the cabbage, cut it in quarters, and remove the core. Cut into chunks that will fit the feed tube. With the slicing disk in place, process with medium pressure to shred. You need 3 cups of shredded cabbage for this dish. Refrigerate any excess for later use.

Switch to the shredding disk, pack the feed tube with bamboo shoots, and process.

With the steel blade in place, put the shrimp into the work bowl and turn the motor on and off quickly once or twice to chop. Avoid overprocessing or you will wind up with shrimp paste. Remove shrimp to a small bowl, combine with the salt and ½ teaspoon cornstarch, and refrigerate.

Slice the pork ⅛ inch thick. With the slicing disk in place, pack the feed tube with slices standing on end and process with firm pressure to shred. Combine the shredded pork with 2 tablespoons soy sauce and 1 teaspoon cornstarch and refrigerate.

ADDITIONAL PREPARATION

Chop the scallions, keeping the white and green

* SUBSTITUTION

2 ounces of Chinese black mushrooms (see page 26) can be substituted. Soak in water for at least 1 hour, discard the stems, pat dry, and cut into shreds. Add to the dish with the bamboo shoots.

parts separate. Rinse the mushrooms and pat dry. Large ones should be sliced, small ones left whole.

COOKING

Cook the noodles in boiling salted water, drain, rinse under cold water to stop cooking, and drain again. Mix in 3 tablespoons of soy sauce and set aside.

Coat the bottom of a frying pan or wok with ½ teaspoon oil and set the pan over medium heat. Beat the egg. When the oil is hot, put in the egg, rotating the pan to spread it as far as it will go and make a thin crepe. When the egg has set, lift the crepe carefully to a cutting board. After it has cooled enough to handle, roll it up tightly and slice with a sharp knife to make thin shreds. Set aside for use as a garnish.

Wipe the wok with a paper towel and put in 2 tablespoons of corn oil. When the oil is hot, add the cabbage and stir-fry 1 minute. Add the bamboo shoots and mushrooms and stir-fry 1 minute more. Remove to a large bowl.

Wipe the wok again and put in ½ tablespoon oil. When the oil is hot, put in the pork and stir-fry until it is cooked through and loses its pink color. Add to the bowl with the cabbage.

Heat another tablespoon oil in the wok and put in the chopped shrimp and scallion whites. Cook, stirring, until the shrimp turn pink, 2 or 3 minutes. Remove to the bowl with the other cooked ingredients, stir the mixture and taste to see if more salt or soy sauce is needed.

Wipe the wok once more, put in the rest of the oil, and set it over medium-high heat. When the oil is hot, put in the noodles, tossing and turning until they are thoroughly heated, then add the cooked ingredients and toss to combine. Continue to cook for a few minutes, until the dish is thoroughly heated. Place the noodles on a large platter, garnish with the scallion greens and the shredded egg crepe.

NOTE

A Teflon-coated pan or wok will be helpful for this dish. This dish can be frozen after it has been cooked, or just the vegetable and meat ingredients can be frozen, to combine later with freshly cooked noodles. Reheat quickly in a pan or wok, not in the oven.

Beef and Noodles
4 to 6 Servings

This recipe is based on a dish from Sze-Chuan, a western province of China noted for its peppery-hot specialties. It is spicy but you can cool the fire by eliminating or reducing the amount of some hot ingredients.

3 pounds stewing beef, such as chuck, partially frozen	4 to 6 dried red peppers (optional)
1 tablespoon cornstarch	½ tablespoon Tabasco sauce (optional)*
2 tablespoons water	
⅓ cup soy sauce	2 tablespoons Red Hot sauce (optional)*
¼ teaspoon anise powder	
1 teaspoon white pepper	1 pound fresh noodles, or packaged spaghetti, linguine, or vermicelli
1 tablespoon sugar	

PREPARATION

With a sharp knife or cleaver, cut the meat into ¾-inch cubes.

Mix the cornstarch and water and set aside.

COOKING

Bring 4 cups of water to a boil in a large pot. Put in the meat and boil for a few minutes. Pour off the water and rinse the meat and the pot. Return meat to the pot with water to cover and bring to a boil. Add soy sauce,

* SUBSTITUTION

Sesame-seed oil (see page 29) with chili can take the place of the Tabasco and Red Hot sauces.

anise powder, pepper, sugar, and dried red peppers. Simmer for 1½ hours. Gradually add the cornstarch mixture to the liquid in the pot to thicken it. Add the Tabasco sauce and the Red Hot sauce, mix well, cover, and keep warm over very low heat.

Cook noodles in boiling salted water. Drain, put in a large bowl, and pour the meat and gravy over them.

NOTE
The beef and gravy freeze very well. To serve, reheat and pour over freshly cooked noodles.

Pork and Noodles
   4 to 6 Servings

This tasty dish is so quick and easy to make it could become one of your busy-day standbys.

2 medium onions	½ teaspoon white pepper
4 to 6 pork chops, cut ¼ to ⅓ inch thick	½ cup chicken broth
⅓ cup soy sauce	1 pound fresh or packaged egg noodles
1½ teaspoons cornstarch	3 tablespoons corn oil

PROCESSING
Peel the onions and cut in half from top to bottom. Stand on end in the feed tube and process with the slicing disk.

ADDITIONAL PREPARATION
Cut the meat away from the bones, trim off the fat, and cut chops into 1-inch pieces. Combine 3 tablespoons soy sauce, ½ teaspoon cornstarch, and the pepper. Marinate the pork in this mixture for 10 minutes, turning once or twice.

Mix the remaining teaspoon cornstarch with the chicken broth and set aside.

COOKING

Cook noodles in boiling salted water. Drain and add 3 tablespoons soy sauce, tossing to distribute evenly.

Heat the oil in a wok or frying pan over medium-high heat. When the oil is hot, put in the pork and turn while cooking until the pieces are brown on all sides. Turn heat to low, cover, and continue cooking 3 minutes (5 minutes for thicker pieces). Uncover, remove the pork to a plate, turn the heat up to medium, and cook the onions in the same pan until tender. (If you prefer very soft onions, cover while cooking.) Slowly add the cornstarch mixture to the onions and cook, stirring, until the sauce thickens. Put noodles in the pan and heat thoroughly while tossing to distribute the sauce. Add the pork pieces, cook one minute more, and serve.

NOTE

You can reheat this dish in a wok or pan.

Chicken and Noodles
4 to 6 Servings

1 small head cabbage*
1 2½ to 3 pound frying or broiling chicken
2 teaspoons salt
1 teaspoon white pepper
1 tablespoon cornstarch

2 tablespoons cold water
1 can (8 ounces) sliced bamboo shoots
1 pound fine noodles, plain or with egg, fresh or packaged

PROCESSING

Discard outer leaves of the cabbage, quarter, and remove the core. Cut lengthwise chunks to fit the feed tube. Shred with the slicing disk, using medium pressure.

* SUBSTITUTION

Chinese cabbage (bok choy) or celery cabbage will improve the flavor of this dish. They are sometimes available in neighborhood supermarkets.

COOKING

Bring 4 cups of water to a boil in a large pot, add the whole chicken with salt and pepper. Bring to a boil again, turn down the heat, and simmer 45 minutes. Put the chicken on a plate, and when it is cool enough to handle, remove the skin and bones and cut the meat into long strips. Meanwhile, continue boiling the chicken broth to reduce it to approximately 2 cups. Combine the cornstarch and water and add slowly to the boiling broth to thicken. Lower heat, add cabbage and bamboo shoots, and cook 1 more minute.

While the broth boils, cook the noodles in boiling salted water and drain. Add the noodles and chicken pieces to the sauce and continue cooking over low heat until the noodles absorb the sauce. Add additional seasoning—salt, soy sauce, or hot sauce—to your taste.

NOTE

Leftovers can be refrigerated for a day or two and reheated in a pan or wok on top of the stove, not in the oven. Do not freeze.

Roast Pork and Noodles
4 to 6 Servings

This is a wonderful way to use leftover roast pork. And it is fast and easy to prepare.

1½ cups roast pork	2 tablespoons corn oil
1 pound fresh noodles or packaged vermicelli	1 teaspoon hot oil (optional)*
3 tablespoons soy sauce	

* SUBSTITUTION

Homemade hot chili oil (see page 28), sesame-seed oil with chili (see page 29), or Red Hot sauce can be substituted for the hot oil.

PROCESSING

Cut the pork into chunks that will fit the feed tube of the processor. With the slicing disk in place, process with light pressure for thin slices.

COOKING

Cook noodles in boiling salted water, drain, add soy sauce, and mix well.

Put the corn oil in a Teflon-coated wok or frying pan over medium-high heat. When the oil is hot, put in the noodles and toss until thoroughly heated. Add the roast pork and hot oil, heat through and serve.

Pan-Fried Noodles
3 to 4 Servings

This is a specialty of the eastern region. Its name in Chinese means "two sides brown," and that gives you an idea of how it is prepared. The noodles are pan-fried until crisp on both sides, then topped with an assortment of delicious ingredients.

4 ounces fresh mushrooms*	2 scallions
½ pound fresh or frozen shrimp, shelled and deveined*	4 ounces fresh snow-pea pods*
1½ teaspoons salt	½ pound fresh or packaged noodles
¾ cup chicken broth	2 tablespoons soy sauce
1 teaspoon cornstarch	⅓ cup corn oil

* SUBSTITUTIONS

Canned mushrooms or Chinese black mushrooms can take the place of fresh mushrooms. King crabmeat, defrosted, can be used instead of shrimp. No stir-frying is required. If fresh pea pods are unavailable, use frozen ones instead.

PROCESSING

Wash the mushrooms, pack in the feed tube with the slicing disk in place, and process with medium pressure to get uniform slices.

ADDITIONAL PREPARATION

Wash the shrimp and split in half or, if they are small, leave whole. Season with ½ teaspoon salt. Mix the chicken broth with the cornstarch. Chop the scallions, keeping the white and green parts separate. Wash the pea pods and remove the stems and strings.

COOKING

Cook noodles in boiling salted water, drain, rinse under cold water, and drain again. Add 2 tablespoons soy sauce and mix well. Place the noodles on a large round dinner plate and pack them tight. Let stand at least an hour to dry out.

Put 1½ tablespoons corn oil in a flat-bottomed frying pan over low heat. When the oil is hot, put in the noodles and rotate the pan so the oil will coat the bottom of the noodles evenly. Pan-fry 4 or 5 minutes. At this point the noodles should hold together like a large pancake. Turn it over and add another 1½ tablespoons corn oil around the edge of the pan rotating again to coat the second side. Cook another 4 or 5 minutes. Both sides should be crisp and brown.

While the noodles are frying, put 2 tablespoons oil in a wok. When the oil is hot, add the snow peas and mushrooms. Sprinkle with the rest of the salt, stir-fry for 1 minute, and remove to a dish. Wipe the wok clean with paper towels.

Put 1 tablespoon corn oil in the wok, and when it is hot, put in the scallion whites and the shrimp. Stir-fry until the shrimp turn pink. Stir the chicken-broth-and-cornstarch mixture and add gradually to the wok with the shrimp. Bring to a boil, and when the sauce has thickened, add the vegetables. Cook for 30 seconds. Pour over the fried noodles, and serve immediately, topped with the scallion greens.

NOTE
When the noodles have dried on the plate, you can store them covered in the refrigerator. The shrimp and sauce can be prepared ahead of time and reheated at the last minute.

Eggs and Noodles
4 to 6 Servings

If you like eggs as much as my husband does, you will be delighted with this dish. Southeast Asians always scramble eggs into their noodles, so I adapted their technique to make my husband happy. It makes an excellent side dish, and it couldn't be simpler.

1 **pound egg noodles, fresh** or **packaged**	3 **eggs** **White vinegar**
3 **tablespoons soy sauce**	**Soy sauce**
3 **tablespoons corn oil**	

COOKING
Cook noodles in boiling salted water. Drain and mix in 3 tablespoons soy sauce. Put 2 tablespoons corn oil in a Teflon-coated wok or pan. When the oil is hot, add the noodles and toss to heat through.

Heat 1 tablespoon corn oil in another pan. Beat the eggs and cook, stirring, until they are set. Combine scrambled eggs with the noodles and serve.

To perk up the flavor, make a sauce of equal amounts of white vinegar and soy sauce and serve on the side.

Noodles with Scallions and Ginger
  4 to 6 Servings

The flavors of scallions and ginger are so compatible they make this dish tasty enough for a banquet. The flavor is improved if you use fresh ginger root and a good oyster sauce.

6 scallions	¼ cup corn oil
1 pound fine egg noodles, fresh or packaged	1 teaspoon ginger powder*
3 tablespoons soy sauce	2 tablespoons Dee's Clam Sauce (recipe below)*

PROCESSING
Cut the scallions the height of the feed tube. With the slicing disk in place, pack the feed tube with the scallions, standing upright, and process with light pressure to chop.

COOKING
Cook the noodles in boiling salted water, drain, and mix in the soy sauce.

Heat the corn oil in a wok or pan. Cook the scallions briefly until they are soft. Add the ginger, then the noodles, and toss, mixing well, until they are heated through. Add the clam sauce and serve.

Dee's Clam Sauce

I developed this sauce to use when oyster sauce is not available.

* SUBSTITUTIONS
Fresh ginger root, peeled and finely minced, then cooked in oil with the scallions, can substitute for the ginger powder and will give a more distinctive flavor (see page 27). If Hop Sing lung oyster sauce is available, use it instead of the clam sauce.

1 cup (8-ounce bottle) clam juice	⅛ teaspoon white pepper
1 tablespoon soy sauce	½ tablespoon sugar
¼ teaspoon salt	1 scallion bulb, chopped
	Dash garlic powder

Combine all the ingredients in a small pan and cook over high heat until the liquid is reduced to half its volume. If it seems a little thin, thicken it with ½ teaspoon cornstarch mixed with a teaspoon of water. Store in the refrigerator in a glass jar.

Noodles with Beef Sauce
4 to 6 Servings

Some people say that Marco Polo brought this recipe back to Italy with him and so originated spaghetti and meat sauce. True or not, it's a delicious dish. I am giving you two versions, one using easily available ingredients, the other an authentic recipe.

2 medium onions	1 pound ground beef
1 can (8 ounces) bamboo shoots	1 tablespoon water
4 ounces fresh mushrooms	3 tablespoons corn oil
3 tablespoons soy sauce	1½ cups chicken broth
3½ teaspoons cornstarch	½ teaspoon Gravy Master
	1 pound noodles

PROCESSING
Cut the onions in quarters and put them in the work bowl with the steel blade. Process with an on-off motion for about 6 to 8 seconds. Remove to a dish. Repeat with the bamboo shoots and then the mushrooms, making sure they are not minced too fine.

ADDITIONAL PREPARATION
Mix 2 tablespoons soy sauce and 2 teaspoons cornstarch with the ground beef.

Mix 1½ teaspoons cornstarch with a tablespoon of water.

COOKING

Put the corn oil in a wok or pan. When the oil is hot, add the beef and cook until it turns brown. Remove to a bowl. Put the chopped onions in the pan and cook until soft. Add the bamboo shoots, mushrooms, beef, and chicken broth, bring to a boil and simmer 5 minutes. Thicken gradually with the cornstarch-and-water mixture. Add the remaining soy sauce and the Gravy Master.

While the sauce is simmering, cook the noodles in boiling salted water. Drain.

Serve the sauce and noodles in separate dishes so each person can combine his own. You can also serve white vinegar, soy sauce, and hot oil in separate little dishes for individual seasoning.

This sauce freezes well in jars.

Authentic Version

½ cup reconstituted Chinese black mushrooms
(2 tablespoons dried; see page 26)
½ cup bamboo shoots
2 scallions
2 teaspoons cornstarch
2 cups plus 2 tablespoons water

½ cup bean sauce (see page 26)
2 tablespoons corn oil
1 pound ground pork
4 tablespoons Hoisin sauce (see page 28)
2 teaspoons sugar

Mince the mushrooms and then the bamboo shoots with the steel blade of the food processor. Chop the scallions. Mix the cornstarch and 2 tablespoons of water.

Bring the bean sauce to a boil in a small saucepan with 2 cups of water, and simmer 5 minutes. While the bean sauce is cooking, heat the corn oil in a wok or deep pan. When it is hot, add the pork and cook until it loses its pink color.

Strain the bean sauce over the pork. (There are

pieces of soybean in the sauce which are quite salty, and I prefer to remove them.)

Add the mushrooms, bamboo shoots, Hoisin sauce, and sugar. Bring to a boil and simmer for 10 minutes. Thicken gradually with the cornstarch mixture. Put in a large bowl, top with chopped scallions, and serve with cooked noodles.

NOTE
This sauce freezes very well.

Noodles with Soup
4 to 6 Servings

The first essential is a flavorful broth. Put about 3 or 4 ounces of cooked noodles in each bowl of soup and then use your imagination. You can add vegetables, seafood, and meat in many combinations, for a delicious bowl of noodles with soup. Here is one example.

4 ounces fresh mushrooms	Dash of white pepper
½ pound lean pork, partially frozen*	2 tablespoons soy sauce
2 scallions	1 teaspoon cornstarch
1 package fresh spinach	4 to 6 cups chicken broth, preferably homemade
½ pound fresh shrimp, cleaned and deveined*	4 cups cooked noodles
½ teaspoon salt	1 can (8 ounces) sliced bamboo shoots

PROCESSING
Wash the mushrooms, pack them in the feed tube with the slicing disk in place, and process with pressure.

Cut the pork into chunks to fit the feed tube and process with pressure to get uniform slices.

* SUBSTITUTIONS
Beef can substitute for the pork, and frozen shrimp or king crabmeat can be used instead of the fresh shrimp.

Remove the slicing disk and put the scallions, cut in 1½-inch pieces, into the work bowl with the steel blade. Chop by turning the motor on and off 2 or 3 times.

ADDITIONAL PREPARATION

Wash and drain the spinach. Cut the shrimp in half and season with the salt and pepper. Combine the pork slices with the cornstarch and soy sauce.

COOKING

Heat 1½ tablespoons corn oil in a wok or pan. Put in the pork and stir-fry until cooked through and brown. Remove to a dish. Add the rest of the oil and stir-fry the shrimp until they turn pink, about 2 or 3 minutes.

Heat the soup in a large pot. When it is boiling, add the noodles, spinach, bamboo shoots, and mushrooms. Bring to a boil again and let it simmer for 2 minutes, stirring to mix the ingredients.

To serve, put a portion of noodles in each bowl. Divide the pork and shrimp equally and place in the bowls. Pour the soup over and sprinkle with chopped scallions.

Cold Tossed Noodles
4 to 6 Servings

This is a delicious treat on hot summer days. You can prepare everything in advance and refrigerate. Cold Tossed Noodles are also excellent for a buffet dinner, because you don't have to worry about keeping them warm. The idea is to present a number of garnishes and side dishes and let everyone combine his own noodle mix—sort of like a salad bar.

½ pound boiled ham

1 pound cooked chicken or turkey

2 cucumbers

1 teaspoon salt

½ cup smooth peanut butter*

½ cup cold strong tea

1 pound fresh bean sprouts

1 pound fresh or packaged noodles

3 tablespoons corn oil

½ cup soy sauce

½ cup white vinegar

½ cup hot oil*

PROCESSING

Slice the ham ⅛-inch thick, stack 4 or 5 slices and place them on edge in the feed tube, with the slicing disk in place. Process with pressure for uniform shreds. Slice the chicken the same way.

Peel the cucumbers, slice in half lengthwise, and scoop out the seeds with a teaspoon. Cut into 2-inch pieces and pack them into the feed tube with the shredding disk in place. The cucumber pieces should lie crosswise in the feed tube, one on top of the other. Process with pressure, and you will get nice long shreds.

ADDITIONAL PREPARATION

Sprinkle salt on the cucumber shreds and let them stand at least 20 minutes in the refrigerator. Drain off the liquid that accumulates.

Put the peanut butter in a small bowl and add the tea gradually to make a smooth paste. Keep it covered.

Pick the tails off the bean sprouts. (This is an optional step, but I think they look and taste better this way.)

* SUBSTITUTIONS

When we first came to the United States, we could not get sesame-seed paste, so I tried substituting peanut butter, and we found we liked it just as much. The tea brings out the flavor, and peanut butter is not as strong as sesame-seed paste. If you use sesame-seed paste, dilute it with a little strong tea or corn oil. Sesame-seed oil with chili can be substituted for the hot oil (see pages 28, 29).

COOKING

Bring about 6 cups of water to a boil and pour over the bean sprouts in a strainer or colander. Drain the sprouts and refrigerate them.

Cook the noodles in boiling salted water. Drain and rinse quickly under cold water. Be sure you do not overcook them. Mix in 3 tablespoons corn oil and store, covered, in the refrigerator.

To serve, place the noodles on a large platter with the ham, chicken, cucumber, and bean sprouts in smaller dishes around it. Put the peanut-butter paste, soy sauce, vinegar, and hot oil in little dishes. Let each person mix his own noodle dish from the array of ingredients.

12
Rice

Rice is the main food staple in China. It accompanies all vegetable and meat dishes, so it is important to cook rice in the right way. However, the "right" way varies in different regions. Easterners prefer their rice soft. In the south they like it hard, with each grain separate. Many times in my household we have had to cook two pots of rice to satisfy everyone's taste.

The method I will show you gives results that seem to be popular with most people. If you like your rice softer or harder, you can adjust the proportions of rice and water.

Fried rice is plain rice stir-fried with meat and other ingredients. It can be served as a side dish or a complete main dish. If you keep some cold cooked rice in your freezer or refrigerator, you can always whip up a quick meal at a moment's notice.

There are two ways to cook fried rice. The traditional method calls for putting the rice in oil, then adding scrambled eggs. My way is to coat the rice with beaten egg before cooking in the oil, which requires less oil. If you are concerned about cholesterol you can use an egg substitute. It will work just as well.

Always make fried rice with *cold* cooked rice if you don't want it to turn out soggy. And never reheat fried rice in the oven. Oven heat dries out the rice; quick top-of-stove cooking preserves the texture.

Plain Rice

One cup of raw rice makes about 2 cups of cooked rice and will serve 2 people. Here are the proportions for making different amounts; the rice-water ratio changes as you increase the amount of rice. All measurements and directions are for long-grain rice.

1 cup rice	3 cups rice
1½ cups water	4 cups water
2 cups rice	4 cups rice
2¾ cups water	5 cups water

Rinse the rice once and pour off the water. Add the correct amount of water to the rice in a deep pot. Set it over medium-high heat and bring it to a boil uncovered. Continue boiling until almost all the water has been absorbed by the rice. Then put the cover on, put the heat on the lowest possible setting, and simmer until each grain is cooked. This will take anywhere from 15 to 45 minutes, depending on the amount of rice you are cooking (15 minutes for 1 cup of rice, 45 minutes for 4 to 5 cups of rice). Fluff with a fork and serve.

It is time-saving and convenient to cook a large quantity of rice and freeze extra portions. Here are two excellent methods for freezing and reheating.

1. Freeze portions of rice in plastic food bags. When you want to use it, empty the rice into a heat-proof bowl, set it on a cake rack in a large, deep pot, and put 1½ inches of water in the bottom of the pot. Cover and set over medium-high heat. Steam for 30 to 45 minutes,

depending on the amount of rice. It will be as fluffy as just-cooked rice.

2. Put portions of rice in seal-a-meal bags, seal, and freeze. When you want to use it, drop the bag in boiling water and boil for 20 minutes. Cut the bag open and serve.

Shrimp Fried Rice
4 Servings

½ pound fresh shrimp, cleaned and deveined*	2 scallions
	2 eggs
¼ teaspoon white pepper	3 cups cold cooked rice
2 teaspoons salt	3 tablespoons corn oil
½ teaspoon cornstarch	1 tablespoon soy sauce

PROCESSING

Put the shrimp into the work bowl with the steel blade and chop in pea-size pieces by turning the motor on and off quickly for 3 to 5 seconds.

ADDITIONAL PREPARATION

Mix the shrimp with pepper, ½ teaspoon salt, and the cornstarch.

Chop the scallions, keeping the white and green parts separate.

Beat the eggs with the remaining salt and stir into the rice. Mix well.

COOKING

Put 2 tablespoons corn oil in a wok or pan and set over medium-high heat. When the oil is hot, add the scallion greens and cook until light brown. Add the rice mixture, stirring and turning to cook thoroughly. The rice grains will become dry and loose. Remove rice from the wok.

* SUBSTITUTION
Frozen shrimp can be used instead of the fresh shrimp.

Wipe the wok with paper towels, put in the remaining tablespoon corn oil, and set over medium-high heat. When the oil is hot, put in the scallion whites, stir a few seconds, and add the shrimp. Stir-fry until the shrimp turn pink, about 2 or 3 minutes. Return the rice to the wok with the shrimp, mix well, add soy sauce, and serve.

NOTE

This dish freezes well. Defrost and reheat in a wok over medium-high heat, stirring and turning to heat quickly. Do not reheat in the oven.

Beef Fried Rice
4 Servings

1 scallion	1 teaspoon cornstarch
1 medium onion	¼ cup chicken broth
2 eggs	½ package frozen green
1½ teaspoons salt	peas*
3 cups cold cooked rice	3 tablespoons corn oil
½ pound (1 cup) ground	1 tablespoon catsup
beef	(optional)*
1 tablespoon soy sauce	

PROCESSING

Cut the scallion in 1½-inch pieces, put in the work bowl with the steel blade, and chop by turning the motor on and off quickly 2 or 3 times.

Peel and quarter the onion and chop the same way.

ADDITIONAL PREPARATION

Beat the eggs with the salt and stir into the rice. Mix well. Combine the ground beef with soy sauce, cornstarch, and chicken broth.

* SUBSTITUTIONS

Use fresh peas when they are available. If you prefer, season the rice with additional soy sauce instead of the catsup.

COOKING

Cook the frozen peas until just tender.

Put 2 tablespoons corn oil in a wok or pan over medium-high heat. When the oil is hot, put in the chopped scallions and cook until light brown. Add the rice mixture, stirring and turning to cook thoroughly. The rice grains will become dry and loose. Remove the rice.

Wipe the wok with paper towels, put in the remaining tablespoon oil, and set over medium-high heat. When the oil is hot, put in the minced onions and cook until they are translucent. Add the ground-beef mixture and stir-fry until the meat burns down. Return the rice to the wok, add the green peas, and combine well. Season with the catsup and serve.

Ham Fried Rice
4 Servings

When I was in China, Ham Fried Rice was a popular snack, eaten morning, noon, or night, whenever hunger pangs struck. I still like it a lot and serve it quite often at home.

2 scallions	3 cups cold cooked rice
6 ounces boiled ham*	2 tablespoons corn oil
2 eggs	1 tablespoon soy sauce
1½ teaspoons salt	

PROCESSING

Cut scallions in 1½-inch pieces, put in the work bowl with the steel blade, and chop by turning the motor on and off quickly, 2 or 3 times.

* SUBSTITUTION

Virginia ham can be used instead of the boiled ham. Smithfield would also be ideal for this dish because it is closest to Chinese ham in flavor. If you use Smithfield ham, which is rather salty, omit the soy sauce.

Cut the ham in 1-inch chunks, put in the work bowl, and mince in the same way.

ADDITIONAL PREPARATION
Beat the eggs with the salt and stir into the rice. Mix well.

COOKING
Put the corn oil in a wok or pan over medium-high heat. When the oil is hot, put in the scallions and cook until light brown. Add the rice mixture, stirring and turning to cook thoroughly. The rice grains will become dry and loose. Add the ham, mix, and cook another minute. Season with soy sauce and serve.

This dish freezes well. Defrost and reheat in a wok over medium-high heat, stirring and turning to heat quickly. Do not reheat in the oven.

Chicken (or Turkey) Fried Rice
4 Servings

Plan on serving this dish the day after you have roasted a chicken or turkey. It is a delicious way to use up leftovers.

2 scallions	1½ teaspoons salt
1 cup cooked chicken or turkey	3 cups cold cooked rice
	2 tablespoons corn oil
2 eggs	1 tablespoon soy sauce

PROCESSING
Cut scallions in 1½-inch pieces, put in the work bowl with the steel blade, and chop by turning the motor on and off quickly 2 or 3 times.

Cut the chicken in 1-inch cubes, put in the work bowl and chop in the same way. Be careful not to overprocess.

ADDITIONAL PREPARATION

Beat the eggs with the salt and stir into the rice. Mix well.

COOKING

Put the corn oil in a wok or pan and set over medium-high heat. When the oil is hot, put in the scallions and cook until light brown. Add the rice mixture, stirring and turning to cook thoroughly. The rice grains will become dry and loose. Add the chicken and soy sauce, and mix well. Cook one more minute to heat through.

NOTE

You can freeze leftover chicken and turkey and defrost when you are ready to prepare fried rice. Or freeze the completed dish. Defrost and reheat quickly in the wok. Do not reheat in the oven.

Roast Pork Fried Rice
4 Servings

Roast Pork was a staple in China, as widely available as ham is in the United States. Each delicatessen had its own secret recipe. The flavor of this dish varies, depending on the roast pork. Shop around for a kind you like, or prepare your own (see page 115).

2 scallions	1 cup roast pork
2 eggs	2 tablespoons corn oil
1½ teaspoons salt	1 tablespoon soy sauce*
3 cups cold cooked rice	

PROCESSING

Cut scallions in 1½-inch pieces, put in the work

* SUBSTITUTION

If available, substitute oyster sauce (see page 29) for the soy sauce.

bowl with the steel blade, and chop by turning the motor on and off quickly 2 or 3 times.

ADDITIONAL PREPARATION

Beat the eggs with the salt and stir into the rice. Mix well. Cut the cooked pork into pea-size pieces.

COOKING

Put the corn oil in a wok or pan and set over medium-high heat. When the oil is hot, put in the scallions and cook until light brown. Add the rice mixture, stirring and turning to cook thoroughly. The rice grains will become dry and loose. Add the roast pork and soy sauce and mix well. Cook for about a minute to heat through.

NOTE

This dish freezes well. Defrost and reheat in a wok over medium-high heat, stirring and turning to heat quickly. Do not reheat in the oven.

Deluxe Fried Rice
4 to 6 Servings

There are so many good things in this dish it can serve as a main course all by itself. It is often presented as the last course in Cantonese banquets. In restaurants the lettuce is usually shredded and mixed into the rice.

2 scallions	1½ teaspoons salt
⅓ cup Alaska king crabmeat	4 cups cold cooked rice
⅓ cup cooked shrimp	1 small head lettuce
⅓ cup cooked chicken or turkey	½ package frozen green peas*
¼ cup boiled or baked ham	3 tablespoons corn oil
3 eggs	1 tablespoon soy sauce*

* SUBSTITUTIONS
Use fresh peas and oyster sauce (see page 29), when available.

PROCESSING

Cut scallions in 1½-inch pieces, put in the work bowl with the steel blade, and chop by turning the motor on and off quickly two or three times.

ADDITIONAL PREPARATION

Cut the crabmeat, shrimp, chicken, and ham in pea-size pieces.

Beat the eggs with the salt and stir into the rice. Mix well.

Wash the lettuce, separate the leaves, and pat dry.

COOKING

Cook the frozen peas according to package directions. Do not overcook.

Put the corn oil in a wok or pan and set over medium-high heat. When the oil is hot, put in the scallions and cook until light brown. Add the rice mixture, stirring and turning to cook thoroughly. The rice grains will become dry and loose. Add the crabmeat, shrimp, chicken, ham, and peas, stirring and turning to combine well. Cook for about a minute to heat through. Season with soy sauce.

To serve, put the rice in the center of a big platter. Arrange the lettuce cups around the edge of the platter. Let each person help himself, spooning rice into the lettuce cups, enclosing and eating with the fingers.

NOTE

This dish freezes well. Defrost, reheat over medium heat, turning and stirring to heat through. Do not reheat in the oven.

Chicken and Rice in the Pot
4 to 6 Servings

This is a home-style southern recipe, energy saving because the rice and chicken are cooked over one source of heat.

1 cup fresh mushrooms	2 tablespoons corn oil
2 cups boneless, skinless raw chicken meat	Dash garlic powder
	2 cups long grain rice
4 tablespoons soy sauce	2¾ cups water
¼ cup chicken broth	1 teaspoon salt
2 teaspoons cornstarch	

PROCESSING

Rinse mushrooms and pat dry. With the slicing disk in place, pack the feed tube with the mushrooms and process with pressure.

ADDITIONAL PREPARATION

Cut the raw chicken into ¾-inch cubes. This will be easier if chicken is partially frozen.

Combine soy sauce, chicken broth, cornstarch, corn oil and garlic powder and pour over the chicken, turning the pieces to coat all sides.

COOKING

Rinse the rice once and place in a large saucepan or Dutch oven. Add water and salt and set over medium heat. Bring to a boil, uncovered, and keep boiling until almost all the water has been absorbed. At this point put the chicken-and-sauce mixture on top of the rice, spreading it evenly to cover the surface. Add the mushrooms. Cover and simmer over low heat for half an hour.

To serve, spoon the chicken and mushrooms into one bowl and put the rice in another.

Authentic Version

Chinese people prefer dark meat and like to serve chicken with the bones because they believe that the meat closest to the bones is the sweetest. So for this dish, they would use a sharp cleaver to cut up chicken legs into 1-inch cubes, with the bone. Also, ¼ cup of Chinese black mushrooms, soaked for an hour, would be used in place of the fresh mushrooms.

Beef and Rice in the Pot
  4 Servings

1 pound flank steak, partially frozen	¼ cup chicken broth
4 tablespoons soy sauce	1 tablespoon cornstarch
1 tablespoon corn oil	⅛ teaspoon white pepper
1 medium onion	2⅛ cups water
1½ cups long grain rice	1 teaspoon salt

PROCESSING

Cut flank steak in chunks to fit the feed tube. With the slicing disk in place, process with firm pressure for uniform slices.

ADDITIONAL PREPARATION

Mix the beef slices with soy sauce, chicken broth, cornstarch, pepper, and corn oil.

Slice onion ¼ inch thick.

COOKING

Rinse the rice once and place in a large saucepan or Dutch oven. Add water and salt and set over medium heat. Bring to a boil, uncovered, and keep boiling until almost all the water has been absorbed. At this point combine the beef and onions and spread them evenly on the rice. Cover, lower heat, and simmer for 15 minutes.

13
Desserts

In China sweets are served as between-meal snacks and at banquets, but never after family dinners. The style is very different from traditional Western cakes, pies, and puddings. There are sweet soups, made with different types of nuts, fruits, and grains, and served hot or cold. There are pastries made with rice flour or tapioca flour or even a kind of sticky rice, called glutinous rice, instead of dough.

Pastries are usually filled with red beans, red dates, or nuts, or a combination. Chinese sweets are less rich and lower in cholesterol than many American desserts, and they combine intriguing flavors you will enjoy tasting. I have chosen a few of the more popular ones for you to experiment with. Don't hesitate to serve these Chinese-style sweets in the American way—at the end of a meal.

Almond Float
4 to 6 Servings

This is a popular Chinese dessert, served as often as Jell-O on American menus. It is light and refreshing, and by using different fruits you can make many variations.

1 package unflavored gelatin*	½ cup evaporated milk
¼ cup sugar	1 tablespoon almond extract
1½ cups water	1 can (8 ounces) Mandarin oranges*

COOKING
Mix gelatin with sugar and water and bring to a boil. Remove from heat. Add evaporated milk and almond extract. Pour into a shallow dish, cool, and refrigerate. Chill the canned fruit at the same time.

To serve, put the fruit with its syrup in individual dessert bowls. Cut the gelatin into small pieces and float them on top of the fruit. Cut any shape you prefer, but try to match the size of the fruit.

NOTE
Cut gelatin pieces will keep for a few days if you refrigerate them in a tightly covered dish.

Sesame-Seed Balls
4 to 6 Servings

When I was a little girl, these deep-fried balls were a frequent treat. Even though the chef never put in

* SUBSTITUTIONS
For a dessert with a different texture, try ¼ ounce agar-agar, a vegetable gelatin (see page 25), as a substitute. For variety, look for Chinese fruits in cans, like lichees, loquats, and lung-ans (see page 28). Canned peaches, pears, pineapple, and fruit cocktail can also be used. Or cut up fresh fruit and add a little water sweetened with honey.

enough sugar to please my taste completely, I ate and ate them. Now that I make them myself, I have adapted the recipe so they come out just the way I like. See if your family can guess what's in them!

2 medium yams	1½ cups corn oil
⅓ cup sugar	½ cup white sesame seeds
3 tablespoons cornstarch*	½ cup powdered sugar

COOKING

Cook the yams in boiling water with their jackets on, until soft. Remove the skins and put through a potato ricer to mash (you'll get about 1 cup) and remove any stringy fibers. While the potatoes are still hot, stir in the sugar and cornstarch. Cool.

Put the oil in a pot over medium-high heat, and while it is heating, start forming the potato balls. Scoop up the mixture with a teaspoon and shape with your fingers. This recipe should make about 30. Roll the balls in sesame seeds and deep-fry them in the hot oil until they turn golden brown. Drain on paper towels. Serve sprinkled with powdered sugar.

Date Pancakes
4 Servings

This is one of my favorite Chinese desserts. Few restaurants serve them, although the recipe is quite simple. You might make extras and keep some in the freezer, as I do.

* SUBSTITUTION
A half cup of glutinous flour or sweet rice flour (see page 29) can take the place of the cornstarch.

4 ounces pitted dates*	2 eggs
¼ cup plus 2 tablespoons sugar	⅔ cup flour
	¼ cup cold water
¼ cup boiling water	¼ cup corn oil

PROCESSING

Put dates and 2 tablespoons sugar in a work bowl with the steel blade. Turn the machine on. While the dates are being chopped, pour boiling water through the feed tube in a stream. Process until dates are puréed. Remove to a dish.

ADDITIONAL PREPARATION

Beat the eggs, add the remaining sugar, and beat until blended. Add flour and mix well. Gradually add the cold water to make a smooth paste. Put 2 tablespoons of the mixture in a small dish and set aside to use as a sealer.

COOKING

Put 1 tablespoon corn oil in a flat-bottomed pan and set over medium heat. When the pan is hot, rotate to coat the bottom evenly. Pour half the batter into the pan and rotate again to cover the pan. When the thin pancake is cooked on one side, remove with a spatula to a plate. Repeat with the other half of the batter to make a second pancake.

Put half of the date pureé in the center of one pancake. Fold it up like a letter envelope and use the reserved batter to seal the flaps. Put the sealed side into the warm frying pan to cook the sealing batter. Repeat with the second pancake.

Put the rest of the corn oil in the pan over medium heat. When the oil is hot, put both pancakes in to pan-fry

*SUBSTITUTION

Chinese date jam in cans can be substituted for the date purée. Or use any of your favorite fruit preserves.

until brown. Turn and pan-fry the other side. Take out and cut each envelope in half to serve.

NOTE
Date Pancakes taste best served hot. You can freeze the filled envelopes in aluminum foil, defrost, and pan-fry them when you are ready to use them.

Watermelon Boat
8 to 10 Servings

This dessert will win you lots of "ahs" and "oohs." It is very pretty and also refreshing and light— ideal for a hot summer day. Do this when you have time and are in the mood to be creative. The whole thing can be prepared a few hours ahead.

½ long watermelon, cut lengthwise	1 cup evaporated milk
2 packages unflavored gelatin*	2 tablespoons almond extract
3 cups water	1 ripe cantaloupe
½ cup sugar	½ ripe honeydew melon

Hollow out the watermelon to make a big bowl, reserving the watermelon meat. Use a sharp knife to make a scalloped or sawtooth border around the edge, and refrigerate.

Remove seeds from the watermelon meat. Cut in chunks and put into the work bowl of the food processor with the steel blade. (Load only to the top of the blade handle.) Process for 2 seconds. Repeat as necessary to chop the remaining watermelon. Put the chopped watermelon through a potato ricer (or strainer) to remove the pulp and retain the juice. Refrigerate the juice in a jar.

* SUBSTITUTION
½ ounce of agar-agar, a vegetable gelatin, can be substituted (see page 25).

Mix the gelatin with water and sugar and bring to a boil. Remove from the heat and add evaporated milk and almond extract. Pour into an oblong baking pan, 8 by 11 inches, cool, and refrigerate.

Cut pieces of cantaloupe and honeydew into diamonds or squares or any shape you prefer. Put the pieces in a bowl, cover, and refrigerate.

To serve, cut the gelatin into pieces matching the cantaloupe and honeydew, lift carefully with a spatula, and place in the hollowed melon half. Shake the jar of watermelon juice and pour it into the melon. Add the cantaloupe and honeydew. The white gelatin, orange cantaloupe, and green honeydew will float in the red melon juice and look delectable.

NOTE

The gelatin can be made 2 or 3 days in advance, but I would not prepare the melons more than a few hours ahead so the fruit will be fresh.

Honeyed Bananas
    4 Servings

This is a different kind of dessert from the others. It is tasty and yet quite easy to make. I developed it in one evening, and I like it so much I can eat it every day.

½ cup dry-roasted peanuts, unsalted	2 tablespoons cornstarch
	6 tablespoons water
2 large bananas	1½ cups corn oil
4 tablespoons flour	⅔ cup honey

PROCESSING

Put the peanuts in the work bowl with the metal blade in place. Turning the motor on and off quickly, process only about 3 seconds to chop.

ADDITIONAL PREPARATION

Peel bananas and cut into 1½-inch pieces. Mix flour, cornstarch, and water to a smooth paste.

COOKING

Heat the corn oil in a saucepan. When the oil is hot, dip a piece of banana in the batter and deep-fry until golden brown. Fry 6 to 8 pieces of banana at one time. Drain on paper towels. Dip the pieces of fried banana in honey and roll in chopped peanuts. Serve immediately.

Although it is best to serve Honeyed Bananas warm, they are nearly as good cold. But do not prepare them too far in advance.

Glazed Pecans
    4 Servings

This is a recipe from the Hunan province. In Hunan walnuts were used rather than pecans, since they were easily available. I prefer pecans, however, because you can buy them in nice unbroken halves. When the nuts are cooked, they become sweet and crunchy, and once you taste them you will find them irresistible. Serve Glazed Pecans over ice cream or sherbet for a delicious dessert, or eat them as candies. In Hunan restaurants they are sometimes served as an appetizer.

1 cup pecans*	⅙ cup water
⅓ cup sugar	1 cup corn oil

COOKING

Put the nuts in a small saucepan with water to cover and bring to a boil. Boil for 5 minutes, then drain off all the water. Add sugar and ⅙ cup water to the nuts. Cook over medium heat for about 10 minutes, until the

* SUBSTITUTION
Use walnuts instead of pecans if you prefer.

sugar melts and the liquid around the nuts gets sticky (or the syrup reaches the soft-ball stage). Remove from the heat and put the nuts on a dish to cool. Separate the nuts so they don't stick together.

Heat the corn oil to 350 degrees F., add nuts and stir while they fry to a golden brown. The sugar coating on the nuts will become caramelized. Lift out the nuts and cool on aluminum foil.

NOTE
Glazed Pecans store well in a jar for 2 or 3 weeks, depending on the weather; humidity makes them soggy.

Flaky Date Pies
12 Small Pies

The original Chinese flaky-type pastry takes a lot of skill and time. I have developed a shortcut to make this recipe so easy you can serve it anytime you want, and I guarantee it will taste almost as good. If you want to compare for yourself, I have also included the authentic version.

1 package (6) Pepperidge Farm frozen patty shells	2 tablespoons chopped walnuts
6 ounces chopped dates*	½ beaten egg
½ tablespoon boiling water	3 tablespoons white sesame seeds

PREPARATION
Thaw the frozen patty shells and divide each in half. Form the dough into 12 round balls. Roll out each ball to a 3-inch round.

Soften the dates with the water and mix in the walnuts. Divide this filling into 12 portions and put a portion

* SUBSTITUTION
Chinese date jam, which comes in cans, can be substituted.

of filling in the center of each round of dough. Gather and press tight, so it looks like a ball, then flatten it slightly. Turn the filled dough so the smooth side of the flattened ball is on top, brush with beaten egg, and sprinkle with sesame seeds. Line up on a cookie sheet.

COOKING
Bake in a 425 degree F. oven for 12 to 15 minutes, until light golden brown.

NOTE
Unbaked pies can be frozen and baked when you are ready to serve them. A toaster oven works fine for this.

Authentic Version

Chinese flaky pastry is actually made with 2 doughs. Dough A is a mixture of 1 cup flour and ½ cup shortening. Dough B is a mixture of 1 cup flour, 3 tablespoons corn oil, and ⅓ cup water. Wrap Dough B around Dough A. Roll out to a rectangular sheet. Fold the sheet of dough in thirds and roll out again to a rectangle measuring 8 by 12 inches. Now roll up the sheet of dough like a jelly roll and cut it into 12 parts. Roll out each part to a 3-inch circle. Enclose the filling, seal, and deep-fry to golden brown.

Steamed Sponge Cake
4 to 8 Servings

In the old Chinese kitchens there were no regulated ovens. All of the breads and cakes were steamed on top of the stove, and sponge cake would be steamed the same way. Steamed cakes are softer and lighter than baked ones. I have added dates and nuts to this cake; eliminate these two ingredients if you want to serve the traditional Chinese version.

¼ cup chopped pitted dates	1½ teaspoons baking powder
¼ cup walnuts	¼ teaspoon baking soda
3 eggs	¼ cup water
¾ cup brown sugar	¼ cup corn oil
1⅓ cups flour	1 teaspoon vanilla extract

PROCESSING

Chop dates and walnuts separately with the steel blade, using on-off motions, for a few seconds.

ADDITIONAL PREPARATION

Grease an 8-inch-square cake pan and line with wax paper. Get ready a large pot that can hold the cake pan on a 2-inch-high cake rack. Fill the pot with 1½ inches water. (If you have a Chinese steamer, fill the bottom with water and set the cake pan on the second tray with the cover on.) Bring the water to a boil. Meanwhile get the batter ready.

Beat the eggs with the brown sugar until the mixture is light and fluffy. This should take about 8 to 10 minutes with an electric mixer. Sift the flour, baking powder, and baking soda together and fold into the egg mixture. Slowly stir in the water.

Heat the corn oil to lukewarm. Add it gradually to the batter. Add the vanilla and fold in the chopped dates and nuts. Pour the batter into the cake pan. Set it over boiling water on the rack to steam, covered, for 50 minutes. Check the water level periodically and add more boiling water as needed. Serve warm, cut in squares.

NOTE

Wrap leftovers in aluminum foil and reheat by steaming for 10 minutes. This cake also freezes very well.

Spun Apples
4 Servings

My students always enjoy this dessert so much they would never forgive me if I didn't include the recipe. It is one dish that must be made at the last minute, and the whole process needs good timing. The syrup plays an important part. You must cook it just to the hard-ball stage, so have a bowl of cold water ready to test it. Make this recipe only when you are serving a small number for dinner, or you will be too frantic to enjoy it.

2 apples, Delicious or McIntosh*	½ cup flour
¾ cup sugar	1½ teaspoons baking powder
½ cup plus 3 tablespoons water	1½ cups corn oil

PREPARATION

Cut apples in quarters and cut each quarter in half. Peel, and remove the core and seeds.

Mix the sugar and 3 tablespoons water in a small saucepan. Empty a tray of ice cubes into a bowl of water and bring it to the dining table.

Mix flour, ½ cup water, and baking powder to a smooth paste and add 1 tablespoons corn oil.

COOKING

Heat the rest of the oil in a pan, and when the oil is hot, dip a piece of apple in the batter, then deep-fry until it is light brown. As you fry the apple pieces, keep them warm on a greased plate in a low oven. When all of the apples have been fried, mix 1 tablespoon hot oil with the sugar-water mixture and put it in a pan over medium-high heat. Keep the syrup boiling until it gets sticky and coats the spoon or chopsticks. This will take about 10 minutes.

* SUBSTITUTION
Bananas can be cooked the same way.

Drop some syrup into a bowl of cold water, and if it forms a hard ball, the syrup is ready. Pour it immediately on the fried apples and bring to the table.

To eat, dip a piece of apple in the ice water. The water will cool the apple and caramelize the syrup. Delicious!

14
Suggestions for Parties

Now that you have mastered the techniques of Chinese cooking and have learned many new dishes, you will certainly want to show off your accomplishments to your relatives and friends. Don't panic! You know you can do it, and the suggestions and menus in this chapter will ensure that your dinners and parties will be brilliantly successful. Just remember the three rules for relaxed entertaining: allow enough time, plan ahead, and organize yourself.

TIME
Give yourself time. Don't have a party on a day's notice. Be kind to yourself so you don't have to rush.

Do things leisurely. When you have enough time to work at a leisurely pace, every step becomes a joy instead of a chore. Do your shopping on one day. Devote another day to food preparation. Save the day of the party for last-minute cooking and for reheating.

Use your freezer. Make room in your freezer so

you can prepare some of the dishes, soups, sauces, fillings, and other parts of the meal ahead of time and store them.

PLANNING

Write out your menu. Plan your menu to suit the preferences of your guests. If you can't research their tastes ahead of time, avoid using too many unfamiliar ingredients. Use your menu as the basis for the next steps.

Assemble your recipes. If they are in different books, copy them on index cards, or at least copy out the ingredients and special instructions (does something have to marinate overnight?), and keep them together.

Make your shopping list. Include everything, even staples you're sure you won't forget—just to be on the safe side.

Make a work schedule. List everything that must be done and assign it to a specific day. List dishes you can do ahead and freeze, those you can store for a day or two in the refrigerator, and last-minute cooking you must leave time for.

ORGANIZE

Check your utensils. Inspect the cooking utensils you will need to make sure they are compatible with your menu. Make sure dishes and flatware are clean and polished. Select a serving dish or platter for each course.

Do a mental run-through. In your mind, go through the whole dinner as though it were happening right that moment. Be sure you have enough room for dishes, drinks, and food.

Expand your counter space. Store everything you won't be needing during the meal, so you will have extra space for food and for used dishes. If you have room, set up a bridge table; you always need more counter space than you think you will.

Dinners for 6 to 8

I am often asked how to serve Chinese food and still be able to sit down with your guests. It isn't really difficult. For a dinner for 6 to 8 people you can serve a hot hors d'oeuvre in the living room with small plates and forks. After that, heat up the soup, warm up cooked dishes, and stir-fry one dish. Or you can serve the soup, remove the soup bowls, and then complete the main dish. A warming tray is handy. And you should choose a dessert that you can prepare ahead of time. Here is a sample of what I mean.

DINNER MENU I

SHRIMP TOAST	DEFROST FROZEN SHRIMP PASTE, SPREAD ON BREAD, DEEP-FRY, AND SERVE AT ONCE IN THE LIVING ROOM.
CHINESE FISH CHOWDER	COOK AHEAD AND REHEAT
BEEF AND BROCCOLI (double recipe)	BROCCOLI PARBOILED OR STIR-FRIED AHEAD; BEEF ALSO HALF-COOKED. AT THE LAST MINUTE REHEAT BROCCOLI, STIR-FRY MEAT, COMBINE.
HAM FRIED RICE	COOKED, REHEATED, KEPT WARM IN OVEN.

BROCCOLI SALAD	SERVED COLD, PREPARED AHEAD OF TIME.
ALMOND FLOAT	PREPARED AHEAD, SERVED COLD.

Now you can see that if you plan your menu carefully about 90 percent of the work can be done ahead. There is only the last-minute reheating and stir-frying. Cutting, marinating, and preliminary cooking are all done the day before or even earlier. You shouldn't be rushed at all.

Here are more sample menus:

DINNER MENU II

DEEP-FRIED WONTONS	FROM FREEZER, LAST-MINUTE DEEP-FRIED.
CHICKEN AND CORN SOUP	REHEAT.
ASPARAGUS COLD MIX	MADE AHEAD, SERVED COLD.
SHRIMP WITH RED SAUCE	LAST-MINUTE STIR-FRY.
MRS. WANG'S TOSSED NOODLES	REHEAT.
DATE PANCAKES	FROM FREEZER, LAST-MINUTE PAN-FRY.

DINNER MENU III

SHRIMP DUMPLINGS	FROM FREEZER, STEAM.
TOMATO AND EGG-DROP SOUP	REHEAT.
FISH FILLET CANTONESE	SAUCE PREPARED AHEAD; POACH FISH AT LAST MINUTE.
BARBECUED SPARERIBS	WARM IN OVEN.

DELUXE FRIED RICE	PREPARE AHEAD. HEAT IN PAN OR WOK, THEN KEEP WARM IN OVEN.
STIR-FRIED CABBAGE	LAST-MINUTE STIR-FRY.
STEAMED SPONGE CAKE	FROM FREEZER, STEAM.

DINNER MENU IV

PAN-FRIED WONTONS	FROM FREEZER, PAN-FRY.
HOT AND SOUR SOUP	REHEAT.
STEAMED CHICKEN WITH SCALLION SAUCE	REHEAT.
NOODLES WITH BEEF SAUCE	REHEAT.
GREEN BEANS SZE-CHUAN	LAST MINUTE.
GLAZED PECANS	FROM JARS.

Dinners for 10 to 12

A dinner of this size is usually called a banquet. In Chinese style we would have one round table large enough to seat everyone. The traditional porcelain dinner sets serve up to twelve and come with different-size bowls for soups like Shark's Fin and dessert soups, small dinner plates and sauce plates. (Since Chinese food is always cut into bite-size pieces you don't need large dinner plates.) Dinner sets also include porcelain spoons for soup, large oval and round serving platters, and a soup tureen. But you don't need all that. You can use your luncheon or cake plates for the main courses, with a second set at hand so you can change plates when dishes are soiled. For the other courses, use your imagination to improvise with what you have on hand.

The true Chinese banquet dinner is a very elaborate affair. During the Ching Dynasty there could easily be more than 20 courses. My father used to tell me about banquets that were so elaborate they took two days to consume. Diners would arrive at a restaurant in the morning to start the banquet. They would play Mah-Jongg, and the courses would be spread out through the whole day. While the chef was preparing the next dish they would play a few games of Mah-Jongg.

Nowadays people's lives have changed. No one can spend that much time in a restaurant or eat that much food. The banquet courses are cut down to ten or so. And a lot of the rare delicacies like bear's paw are hard to get. So today's menus are different—and healthier as well.

I have developed four banquet menus for you to try. The first two are fairly easy. Serve the hors d'oeuvres and soup first. Remove the dishes. Serve the cold dishes while you reheat and do last-minute cooking. Then you can sit down with your guests.

BANQUET MENU I

SHRIMP TOAST	PASTE FROZEN, LAST MINUTE. DEEP FRY.
MOCK-MELON SOUP	REHEAT.
BROCCOLI COLD MIX	COLD.
RADISH FLOWERS	COLD.
CHICKEN COOKED IN SOY	COLD.
ROAST PORK	COLD.
STIR-FRIED SHRIMP SHANGHAI STYLE	LAST-MINUTE STIR-FRY.
BARBECUED BEEF	PREPARE AHEAD. LAST-MINUTE BROIL.
NOODLES WITH SCALLIONS AND GINGER	REHEAT.
ZUCCHINI	REHEAT.
SESAME-SEED BALLS	REHEAT.

BANQUET MENU II

SPARERIBS	PREPARE AHEAD, BROIL.
CHICKEN AND HAM SOUP	REHEAT.
STEAMED CHICKEN CHILLED IN GELATIN	COLD.
BROCCOLI SALAD OR ASPARAGUS COLD MIX	COLD.
COLD TOSSED NOODLES	COLD.
STEAMED WHOLE FISH	STEAMED 15 MINUTES AHEAD.
BEEF AND SNOW-PEA PODS	LAST-MINUTE STIR-FRY.
EGG CRESCENTS	REHEAT.
FLAKY DATE PIES	FROM FREEZER, REHEAT.

The following two sample menus are more elaborate. After the cold dishes you should serve one dish at a time.

BANQUET MENU III

ASPARAGUS COLD MIX	COLD.
PICKLED CABBAGE	COLD.
CHICKEN WINGS COOKED IN SOY	COLD.
ROAST PORK	COLD.
CRABMEAT AND MUSHROOM SOUP	REHEAT.
SHRIMP TOAST	PASTE FROZEN, LAST-MINUTE DEEP-FRY.
SLICED CHICKEN WITH SNOW PEAS	LAST-MINUTE STIR-FRY.
MO SHU PORK AND MANDARIN PANCAKES	MADE AHEAD, REHEAT

STIR-FRIED SCALLOPS WITH WATER CHESTNUTS	LAST-MINUTE STIR-FRY.
CRISPY DUCK WITH STEAMED ROLLS	MADE AHEAD. BROIL DUCK, STEAM BUNS.
STEAK CANTONESE	LAST-MINUTE STIR-FRY.
FILLET OF FISH CANTONESE	REHEAT SAUCE. LAST-MINUTE POACHING OF FISH.
SPUN APPLES (or HONEYED BANANAS)	LAST MINUTE.

BANQUET MENU IV

CHOPPED SPINACH SALAD	COLD.
SWEET-AND-SOUR CAULIFLOWER	COLD.
STEAMED CHICKEN CHILLED IN GELATIN	COLD.
DEEP-FRIED SPARERIBS	COLD.
HOT AND SOUR SOUP	REHEAT.
DEEP-FRIED SHRIMP BALLS	LAST-MINUTE DEEP-FRY.
DICED CHICKEN AND CASHEWS	LAST-MINUTE STIR-FRY.
SHREDDED BEEF WITH BEAN SPROUTS	LAST-MINUTE STIR-FRY.
STIR-FRIED SHRIMP WITH WATER CHESTNUTS	LAST-MINUTE STIR-FRY.
PEKING DUCK WITH MANDARIN PANCAKES	ROASTED. STEAM PANCAKES.
CURRIED BEEF	REHEAT.
DELUXE FRIED RICE, OR MRS. WANG'S TOSSED NOODLES	REHEAT.
STEAMED WHOLE FISH	STEAMED.

| FLAKY DATE PIES | FROM FREEZER, REHEAT |
| WATERMELON BOAT | PREPARE AHEAD. |

If you can do the last banquet with little strain, you are a graduate! Good luck.

Buffet Dinners

When you are entertaining more than twelve people, it is best to serve buffet style. Then you don't have to worry if you have one more or one less guest. People help themselves, and there is a pleasantly casual atmosphere. One or two warming trays will be most helpful—in fact *any* device that can keep a dish warm for about 30 minutes will be useful. But I have served buffet dinners with no warming devices, and they still came out beautiful—because the food disappeared before it could get cold! Here are four sample buffet menus.

BUFFET MENU I
DEEP-FRIED WONTONS
SWEET-AND-SOUR
  PORK
ASPARAGUS COLD MIX
STEAMED CHICKEN
  WITH HOT SAUCE
STIR-FRIED SHRIMP
  WITH WATER
  CHESTNUTS
BEEF FRIED RICE
TASTY CAULIFLOWER
ALMOND FLOAT

BUFFET MENU II
SESAME-SEED PUFFS
CHOPPED SPINACH
  SALAD
CHICKEN COOKED IN
  SOY
BEEF SOONG
ROAST PORK
SHRIMP FRIED RICE
STIR-FRIED CABBAGE
HONEYED BANANAS

BUFFET MENU III
CURRIED CRESCENTS
BROCCOLI COLD MIX
RADISH FLOWERS
CHICKEN CUBES WITH
    ONIONS
BEEF AND BROCCOLI
CHINESE SPARERIBS
RED-COOKED FISH
CUCUMBER EASTERN
    STYLE
GLAZED PECANS

BUFFET MENU IV
SPRING ROLLS
PICKLED CABBAGE
CHICKEN WITH HAM
CURRIED BEEF
EGG CRESCENTS
STIR-FRIED SHRIMP
WATERCRESS
STEAMED SPONGE

CAKES

Outdoor Barbecue

Many Chinese dishes adapt beautifully to cooking outdoors. It is easiest to precook most of the courses and then do the reheating and browning on the outdoor grill. Here is a sample menu.

BARBECUED BEEF
CRISPY CHICKEN
    WINGS AND LEGS
SPARERIBS

A NOODLE OR RICE
    DISH
A COLD SALAD
A HOT VEGETABLE
    DISH
WATERMELON BOAT

Teenage Party

These dishes are fun to eat and not too sophisticated for most young people to enjoy.

BEEF SOONG
SPARERIBS
DEEP-FRIED WONTONS

FRIED RICE OR COLD
    TOSSED
NOODLES

Children's Party

This menu should delight youngsters, and won't seem unfamiliar to them at all.

WONTON SOUP   MRS. WANG'S TOSSED
SPARERIBS   NOODLES

Cocktail Parties

Since everything in the hors d'oeuvres chapter can be prepared ahead and frozen, with good planning you can have all the work for your cocktail party done in advance. On the day of the party just do the last-minute cooking and reheating. Some party suggestions:

Choose a variety of hors d'oeuvres that use different cooking techniques. For instance, if you plan to serve Steamed Shrimp Dumplings, do not serve Meat-Filled Steamed Buns as well.

Deep-Fried Wontons always make a big hit at parties. With a miniature electric deep-fryer, which maintains a steady temperature, you can let guests deep-fry their own.

Arrange other hot hors d'oeuvres on a warming tray.

For variety—and for vegetable lovers—include one or two salads with the hors d'oeuvres. Radish Flowers, Cucumber Fans, and Sweet-and-Sour Cucumbers would all be good choices to add balance to your menu.

Here are some suggested menus:

COCKTAIL PARTY   COCKTAIL PARTY
  MENU I   MENU II
DEEP-FRIED WONTONS   SHRIMP TOAST
STEAMED SHRIMP   PAN-FRIED WONTONS
  DUMPLINGS   SESAME-SEED PUFFS
CURRIED CRESCENTS   SWEET-AND-SOUR
RADISH FLOWERS   CAULIFLOWER

COCKTAIL PARTY
  MENU III
SPRING ROLLS   STEAMED BUNS
SCALLION PIES   CUCUMBER FANS
MEAT-FILLED

Suggestions for Quantity

When you are entertaining, it is good to be on the safe side and have leftovers rather than not enough food, especially if you don't know each person's appetite. For the main course allow at least 6 ounces of meat, poultry, or seafood for each person. If you have more than one main course, then the combined total of meat, poultry, or seafood in all of the dishes should be at least 6 ounces per person.

At banquet dinners, where you have a number of main courses, each person will probably try only a tablespoonful or two of each dish, so you don't have to make a huge amount of each. Just one batch of any recipe in this book should be enough.

For barbecues, allow one-half to three-quarters pound of meat for each person, because fresh air improves the appetite.

Portions at teenage parties will depend on the group. Girls generally eat less than boys.

For children's parties portions should be small. Children are more interested in playing than in eating anyway—and no mother wants her child to be stuffed with food.

Index

Index